THE 6 PRINCIPLES

GRADES K-12

FOR EXEMPLARY TEACHING OF ENGLISH LEARNERS®

TESOL International Association
Writing Team
Deborah J. Short, *Lead Writer*
Helene Becker
Nancy Cloud
Andrea B. Hellman
Linda New Levine

FOREWORD **BY JIM CUMMINS**

This book has a companion website. Go to **www.the6principles.org/K-12** for additional resources.

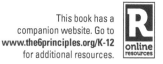

www.tesol.org/bookstore

TESOL International Association
1925 Ballenger Avenue
Alexandria, VA 22314 USA
www.tesol.org

Group Director, Content and Learning: Myrna Jacobs
Copy Editor: Anita Draper
Cover and Interior Design: Kirsten Ankers, Citrine Sky Design
Layout: Capitol Communications, LLC
Printing: Gasch Printing, LLC

ISBN 978-1-945351-30-3
Library of Congress Control Number 2017964569

Recommended citation:
TESOL International Association (TESOL). (2018). *The 6 principles for exemplary teaching of English learners: Grades K–12*. Alexandria, VA: Author.

BULK PURCHASES
Quantity discounts are available for workshops and staff development.
Visit https://bookstore.tesol.org/ for more information.

CONTENTS

CHAPTER 1

CHAPTER 2

CHAPTER 3

CHAPTER 4

CHAPTER 5

FOREWORD

I t is a privilege to write a foreword to this immensely valuable book. The 6 Principles for exemplary teaching of English learners elaborated in these pages provide an evidence-based foundation for schools to examine their own instructional practice and work collaboratively with colleagues, parents, and policymakers to enable English learners to acquire strong social and academic language proficiency. A major strength of the book is its inclusion of the entire school community—administrators, English language teachers, content teachers, school librarians, guidance counselors, and other groups of educators—within the scope of exemplary teaching of English learners. As noted in Chapter 1, most of these education professionals have not had opportunities in their preservice education to access the knowledge base and instructional expertise necessary to work effectively with English learners. The detailed discussion in Chapter 5 of concrete ways in which these various groups of educators can apply the 6 Principles opens not just a culture of shared responsibility within the school, but also a culture of shared opportunity. As our expertise to work effectively with diverse learners expands, so too does our sense of affirmation as *educators*.

An additional strength of the book is the way in which it highlights the instructional implications of well-established research findings that are frequently overlooked in teaching English learners. For example, it is now well-established that bilingualism represents a positive force in children's cognitive and academic development, particularly when literacy is developed in both languages. However, in classroom contexts where multiple languages are represented, many educators have been unsure about how to engage students' multilingual repertoires. In response to this uncertainty, the classroom vignettes and instructional suggestions throughout this book illustrate how teachers, school librarians, and other professionals can mobilize students' home languages as cognitive resources and instructional tools to enrich the learning of all students.

Another significant emphasis throughout this book is on the importance of encouraging English learners to become avid readers, ideally in both English and their L1. There is extensive research evidence regarding the impact of print access and literacy engagement on the development of students' reading comprehension skills (e.g., OECD, 2010). As noted in Chapter 2, students who read extensively "encounter more words and meet each word more frequently, which can result in a larger vocabulary and deeper word knowledge." Unfortunately, this research was largely ignored in reading policies instituted under the No Child Left Behind legislation that operated between 2002 and 2015 (Cummins, 2007).

The importance of promoting active literacy engagement is illustrated in the Programme for International Student Assessment (PISA), an international assessment initiative involving more than 70 countries and hundreds of thousands of 15-year-old students conducted by the Organisation for Economic Cooperation and Development (OECD) over the past 20 years. The PISA research has consistently shown that reading engagement is a stronger predictor of reading achievement than students' socioeconomic status (SES). Furthermore, the OECD (2010) reported that there was about a one-third overlap between the negative effects of low SES and the positive effects of reading engagement. The implication is that schools can potentially 'push back' about one-third of the negative effects of socioeconomic disadvantage by ensuring that students have access to a print-rich environment and become actively engaged with literacy.

This finding assumes relevance in the present context because a large proportion of English learners come from lower-income communities with significantly less access to print in their schools and homes than is the case for students from middle-income communities (e.g., Duke, 2000). Immersion of these students in a literacy-rich environment from the day they enter school is a powerful tool in accelerating their academic catch-up trajectory. *The 6 Principles for Exemplary Teaching of English Learners: Grades K–12* suggests multiple strategies both for engaging parents as partners in this process and creating a culture of literacy engagement throughout the school.

My expectation is that this lucid and inspirational book will act as a catalyst for a process of collective pedagogical inquiry in schools across the United States and internationally. Obviously, all schools operate in broader policy contexts that enable and constrain organizational and pedagogical initiatives to varying degrees. However, within schools, educators always have choices — degrees of freedom within which we can chart directions that reflect and shape our identities as educators. This book charts the landscape in ways that enable us to embark confidently on that journey.

Jim Cummins
University of Toronto

References

Cummins, J. (2007). Pedagogies for the poor? Re-aligning reading instruction for low-income students with scientifically based reading research. *Educational Researcher, 36*, 564–572.

Duke, N. (2000). For the rich it's richer: Print experiences and environments offered to children in very low- and very high-socioeconomic status first-grade classrooms. American Educational Research Journal, 37, 441–478.

OECD. (2010). *PISA 2009 results: Learning to learn—Student engagement, strategies and practices (Volume III)*. Paris: Author. Retrieved from http://www.oecd.org/dataoecd/11/17/48852630.pdf

PREFACE

In a world where people are always on the move and the globalization of society leads us to interact regularly with a diverse group of neighbors, coworkers, shopkeepers, online friends, and even strangers, we all learn a little bit about language and culture every day. Sometimes these interactions are unexpected and delightful; sometimes they are deliberate and planned. As our lives touch others, others' lives touch us. Our interactions are most fruitful when supported by clear communication, respect, and cross-cultural understanding.

TESOL International Association is a community of professionals devoted to nurturing these three factors by means of its mission to advance the quality of English language teaching through professional development, research, standards, and advocacy. Our mission is particularly noteworthy because the number of English learners worldwide is estimated to reach about 2 billion by 2020 (British Council, 2013); and, increasingly, people learning English as a lingua franca more often interact with non-native speakers of English than with native speakers. Much of the information on the internet is posted in English, and English is the most widely used language for international business (Neeley, 2012; W3Techs, 2017). For these reasons, effective English language teaching is critical.

In 2016, TESOL celebrated its 50th anniversary—a remarkable achievement—with close to 12,000 members representing 155 countries and 116 affiliates worldwide. The educational setting has changed since 1966 when TESOL was founded. What we know about teaching and learning has evolved. Our teachers do more than teach conversational skills and basic reading and writing. Our classrooms look different, with new technologies; a broader array of instructional materials; desks, tables and chairs set up to foster interaction; and more. Yet our students' desire to learn hasn't changed.

TESOL's 50th anniversary was a time for both reflection and future planning. TESOL took the occasion to articulate a vision and a set of universal principles that hold the promise of effective education for English learners. Over the years, TESOL has developed standards for a number of purposes. These include pre-K–12 English language proficiency standards, standards for pre-K–12 teacher preparation programs and for short-term TEFL/TESL certificate programs, standards for teachers of adult ESL and EFL learners and for their programs, standards for using technology in instruction, and guidelines for developing EFL professional teaching standards. These standards represent broad statements of skills and conceptual knowledge that teachers or learners should have as the result of a course or program. However, *how* a learner would gain the skills and knowledge has not been the focus of these documents.

This book aims to fill that gap by offering a targeted look at the six core principles of exemplary teaching:

1. Know your learners.
2. Create conditions for language learning.
3. Design high-quality lessons for language development.

4. Adapt lesson delivery as needed.

5. Monitor and assess student language development.

6. Engage and collaborate within a community of practice.

With these principles, this book brings to life the underlying linkages among TESOL's core values, standards, position statements, and other publications. The 6 Principles are research-based and set a foundation for teachers and learners to be successful in a variety of program types. The principles are applicable for classrooms focused on English as a second or new language or English as a foreign language. They will serve educators of children and adults, dual language learners, emerging bilinguals, and multilingual students.

The 6 Principles for Exemplary Teaching of English Learners: Grades K–12 will be the first in a series of TESOL books. This volume lays out important information that teachers should know about English language development, along with the 6 Principles and practical examples of how these principles can be enacted in classrooms. To have a coherent and consistent focus for the practices that we explicate, we decided that this first book would reflect K–12 classrooms in the United States. Many of the examples and suggestions, however, will transfer easily to other types of classrooms. Future books will show, for example, how the 6 Principles can be implemented by educators of adults learning English and by teachers of young learners in countries where English is a foreign language. Additional resources, such as webinars and online courses, will be designed to help teachers and other educators apply these standards in their specific contexts.

Audience

Teachers of English learners in K–12 classrooms are the primary audience for this book. These educators include

- ESL/ELD, bilingual, and dual language teachers (subsequently, for brevity, "English language teachers") in self-contained, co-taught, or resource classrooms;
- elementary grade-level teachers and secondary content teachers; and
- special educators, reading teachers, and teachers of elective courses like music, art, and technology.

Some of these teachers may not view themselves as teachers of English, but they are. They provide direct instruction to students learning English as a new language even if their subject is grade 3 math, middle school social studies, or high school biology. They are models of proficient use of the language; they incorporate the four language skills of reading, writing, listening and speaking in their instruction; and they expect learners to demonstrate their knowledge through these skills too. All teachers must help develop the students' academic English skills while supporting their growing knowledge base in the content areas. For English learners to have access to challenging, grade-level curricula and be successful in school, teachers must understand how second language development occurs and apply that understanding to their lesson designs and assessments. They must also teach in culturally responsive ways that value the learners' languages and heritages.

Secondary audiences for the book include

- school and district administrators;
- instructional coaches;
- other school or district personnel, such as curriculum directors, guidance counselors, and reading specialists, and
- teacher educators and professional developers.

Administrators and coaches have a leadership role in their schools or districts and should help the teachers with whom they work understand the importance of knowing one's learners and how best to instruct them. They are also involved in creating the conditions for learning and thus need to know how to support language development while meeting curriculum goals and standards. Other personnel play additional roles in students' lives, from planning their academic schedules to supporting their wellness to selecting instructional materials. Teacher educators and professional developers can use this book to introduce preservice teachers to the 6 Principles and to help inservice teachers add to or refine their current practices.

Besides using the 6 Principles to guide instruction, school-based educators can use the book to evaluate their school or district programs. As part of school improvement efforts, this book can serve as a tool to drive reform, confirming positive aspects of programs and practices already in place and identifying those that might merit change. The book is designed to generate thoughtful discussion and reflection among educators who serve English learners.

Overview

The book is organized in five chapters:

Chapter 1: A Vision for Exemplary English Language Teaching lays out TESOL's vision for exemplary teaching of English learners, along with the rationale for the U.S. K–12 focus of this book, and introduces the 6 Principles.

Chapter 2: What Teachers Should Know about English Language Development to Plan Instruction summarizes the main factors of second language learning as they apply to K–12 settings in the United States and identifies what teachers should know in order to provide developmentally appropriate instruction and build on students' linguistic and cultural assets, as called for by the 6 Principles.

Chapter 3: The 6 Principles for Exemplary Teaching of English Learners is the cornerstone of the book. It explains the 6 Principles in detail and grounds them in research. For each principle, it identifies a broad range of K–12 instructional practices that guide teachers as they get to know their learners, set up a classroom that promotes student interaction, craft lessons that integrate language and content, modify their lesson delivery on the spot if students struggle, assess student language development, and participate in the school community of practice.

Chapter 4: Additional Roles for Teachers of English Learners describes the various roles that teachers of English learners play in educational contexts outside the classroom. Teachers can function as change agents when they (a) advocate for English learners; (b) act as liaisons among families, communities, and the school system; and (c) serve as resources to other teachers and administrators on instruction, assessment, curriculum design, scheduling and programming, professional development, and so forth.

Chapter 5: Establishing a Culture of Shared Responsibility suggests ways in which school and district administrators, instructional coaches, and other specialists can apply the 6 Principles in their spheres beyond the classroom. All professionals can work together to ensure that English learners receive quality programs and services designed to support their language development needs and foster educational success in a positive, welcoming school climate.

Going Forward

The TESOL profession has much to offer the world in expertise in English language teaching and support for multilingualism and cross-cultural communication. An action agenda resulting from the "Summit on the Future of the TESOL Profession," held in 2017, calls for TESOL professionals to draw on the knowledge, experience, and expertise that they have and be involved in the development and implementation of language policies, practices, and research at local and national levels.

This book complements those efforts and represents a first step in defining what educators need to know in order to teach English learners effectively. It explores where our profession is now and how we want to advance in the future. It defines the best practices for our classrooms, and how to advocate for our students and their families and promote the learning of English while respecting and affirming all languages and cultures.

Deborah J. Short
Helene Becker
Nancy Cloud
Andrea B. Hellman
Linda New Levine
TESOL International Association Writing Team

Acknowledgments

Educators around the world strive to implement best practices in English language development with a myriad of learners in diverse contexts. They have contributed to our understanding of second language learning and teaching. We are grateful to them for sharing their experiences with us through print resources and personal connections. We thank the TESOL Board of Directors and Central Office staff for their ongoing support of the 6 Principles initiative. We would particularly like to acknowledge Myrna Jacobs, Director of Publishing and Product Development; Rosa Aronson, former TESOL Executive Director; Christopher Powers, current Executive Director; John Segota, Associate Executive Director; and Valerie Novick, Professional Relations Manager, for their vision and shepherding of the writing process. Anita Draper has strengthened the text with her careful editing. We are thankful that Karen Woodson, Sherry Blok, Christel Broady, and Ximena Uribe-Zarain were able to provide assistance in some of the chapters, and Jim Cummins deserves our sincere gratitude for writing the Foreword.

We very much appreciated the insights and productive feedback from the reviewers who took time from their busy schedules to respond to the earlier drafts of this book. Some reviewers are members of our TESOL International community, and others are educators from the bilingual and general education fields. All care about our learners and their teachers, and they have helped us write a better book.

Misty Adoniou	Andy Curtis	Andrea Honigsfeld	Judith O'Loughlin
Rosa Aronson	Ester de Jong	Adrienne Johnson	Luis Quan
Angela Bell	Margo DelliCarpini	Gabriela Kleckova	Sarah Sahr
Jeremy Borland	Luciana C. de Oliveira	Gilda Martinez-Alba	Shawn Slakk
Robyn Brinks Lockwood	Anne Marie Foerster Luu	Kia McDaniel	Josie Yanguas
Christel Broady	Fred Genesee	Denise Murray	
Margarita Calderon	Margo Gottlieb	David Nunan	

Dedication

We dedicate this book to our friend and colleague, Dr. Anna Uhl Chamot (1934–2017), with deep appreciation for her years of service, research, writing, and professional development on behalf of English learners and their educators.

1 A VISION FOR EXEMPLARY ENGLISH LANGUAGE TEACHING

Ms. Tejada opened the door to see her daughter and three classmates.

"Mami, estos son mis amigos de la escuela," said Gabriela. "Ricky, Chantal, y John. Estamos trabajando en un proyecto."

"Welcome," said Ms. Tejada, "Please come in. What project are you working on?"

The young teens entered, and John turned to Gabriela's mother. "We are working on a project about Darwin's journey around the world. We have to make a map of his trip, tell why he made the journey, identify challenges and solutions, and describe different groups of people he met and different things he saw."

Ricky continued, "We have to tell about his discoveries too."

Ms. Tejada said, "Goodness, that's a lot of work. How will you do all that?"

"Watch us, Mami," said her daughter.

The teens moved into the dining room and opened their tablets from the school. Chantal spread out a printed world map. She placed a toy boat on the south coast of England and took a picture. Ms. Tejada saw her draw a route to the Canary Islands in red marker, place the boat there, and take another picture. Chantal did the same for the Cape Verde islands. "Donde, uh, where next?" she asked John.

John said, "Remember how to Google, ah, la carte? Let me show you." He helped Chantal find a web page with the route of Darwin's ship.

To her mother, Gabriela said, "Chantal es de Haití. Ella es nueva y está aprendiendo inglés."

Her mom replied, "I'm glad you all are helping her."

Ricky, Gabriela, and John were looking at different web pages and taking notes in their notebooks. Occasionally they took a screenshot. Ms. Tejada watched for a while.

Ricky asked, "Did you know Darwin went to South America? He studied birds—finches—and saw things that were the same and different about them."

John turned to Gabriela, "Come here and help me read this article. It's in Spanish about the Galapagos Islands."

The teens worked for another hour. Before leaving, they looked over the pictures they had taken. Chantal showed the map photos, and the boys asked her to tell them the places where the boat was in each one. They helped her say the names of the towns and practice sentences like "The Beagle sailed to Cape Verde," and "The Beagle is in Cape Town." Gabriela then pointed at some of the bird pictures and said, "Look at the beaks. This one is long. That one is short and thick. Darwin noticed the beaks changed to match the food the birds ate."

As they were preparing dinner, Ms. Tejada asked her daughter to tell her more about the project. "When I was in school," she said, "we would read some books and write a report. We'd work by ourselves."

Gabriela explained, "This is better, Mami. We are working on this in our science and geography classes. For the final project, we are going to do a screencast about Darwin's voyage. It's kind of *like a PowerPoint with sound. We have to put the photos we take with the tablet into a computer program, and then we can record information about each one. What's good is that we can record over what we say if we make a mistake. Each one of us has to speak part of the time. That's why we were helping Chantal practice. But we have four more days before we have to finish."*

Gabriela went on to explain how the teachers on her middle school team were supporting the project. Mr. Mohan, the ESL teacher, co-teaches with the science teacher, Ms. Kitima. In class, he explains the vocabulary and helps when they read texts. He helps them form sentences to express their ideas when they have to speak or write. In their current unit, Ms. Kitima is teaching them about biodiversity. She uses a lot of photographs and video clips, and they did an experiment where they had to try to get food that birds eat—worms in soil, seeds on branches, and nuts on the ground—using different utensils, like tweezers, nutcrackers, and straws. Mr. Gándara, the social studies teacher, has bookmarked web pages for the geography tasks of the project. He has found some in Spanish and French, besides English. He also reads aloud parts of the diary that Darwin kept when he was sailing and explains what Darwin was finding. In ESL class with Mr. Mohan, they read some of the diary entries closely and take notes.

"John no está en ESL pero estudia francés. Él puede ayudar a Chantal un poco," Gabriela concluded.

"You make a good team," said her mom.

We have written this book to share TESOL's vision for exemplary teaching of English learners and to introduce the 6 Principles—a core set of principles that should undergird any program of English language instruction. The pressing interest in learning English around the world creates a need for a common understanding of second language learning theory and effective instructional and assessment design. We want to dispel misperceptions about second language acquisition and help educators understand contemporary ideas about pedagogy so that they will make informed decisions about the teaching and learning process. We hope that this book will empower teachers of English learners to share their expertise with colleagues at the local levels and to reflect critically on their current practices.

TESOL believes that all languages and cultures have equal worth and promotes multilingualism and multiculturalism. Respect for all languages and cultures is a core value. We recognize that many people around the world want to learn English for a variety of personal, academic, and economic reasons, so TESOL, as the leading organization of English language teaching professionals, offers its best guidance here, based on research findings and practitioner knowledge.

The vision, 6 Principles, and accompanying practices are applicable to all contexts and all audiences. However, for the reasons outlined below and to illustrate the principles with a cohesive narrative in this first book of a series, we have set out the practices for learning English as a new language in elementary and secondary schools in the United States. The vignette that opens this chapter is a snapshot of effective instruction that enables students to collaborate around an academically challenging project, using their language resources and instructional materials, and developing academic English.

The Need for the 6 Principles in the United States

The 6 Principles are universal and establish the foundation for exemplary teaching of English learners. They are particularly relevant to the educational context in the United States in the 21st century for several academic and sociocultural reasons:

English learners are the fastest growing subgroup of students in U.S. schools, and their numbers increase each year. English learners represented close to 10 percent of the population in pre-K–12 schools in the 2014–15 school year, and the percentage is expected to reach 20 percent by 2020 (National Center for Education Statistics, 2016). Educators report that the number of students who struggle with the academic language of school is considerably higher than the number of learners in English language support programs because some learners who have exited the programs have not attained all the academic English skills that would allow them to participate successfully in all their content courses.

Many elementary grade-level and secondary content area teachers have not had all the preparation they need to teach English learners effectively. English as a second language (ESL) teachers (also known as English language development [ELD] teachers), bilingual teachers, and dual language teachers (all subsequently identified inclusively as "English language teachers," for brevity) are well-trained to teach in and about English. But essential courses on second language acquisition, ESL techniques for integrating language and content, and cross-cultural communication are not the norm for others studying to be teachers in U.S. schools (López, Scanlan, & Gundrum, 2013; National Academies of Sciences, Engineering, and Medicine, 2017). Often school districts find that they need to provide inservice training in these areas. A recent report found that only 24 percent of elementary teacher preparation programs taught any strategies for teaching reading to English learners to their teacher candidates (National Council on Teacher Quality, 2015).

National standards for teacher education institutions recognize that teachers need to understand how to work with diverse learners, including English learners, and that they should keep students' culture and language differences in mind to create inclusive learning plans (see www.caepnet.org/standards/introduction). However, the standards do not outline the specific coursework that should be taught or the depth of treatment. Given the demands of state content standards and the high numbers of English learners in our schools, future teachers need resources like the 6 Principles for details on how to teach the academic language and literacy skills necessary for their subject areas to students who are not yet proficient in English.

Acronyms Associated with English Learners or Programs

EL/ELL	English learner/English language learner
ELD	English language development
ELP	English language proficiency
ENL	English as a new language
EO	English only (refers to native speakers of English)
ESL	English as a second language (refers to students, classes, programs, and the professional field)
ESLWD	English as a second language student with a learning disability (also known as dually identified student)
ESOL	English speakers of other languages (refers to students)
ESOL	English to speakers of other languages (refers to programs)
FEP	Fully English proficient/Fluent English proficient
L1	First language (also home language, primary language, native language)
L2	Second language
LEP	Limited English proficient (used in some federal and state regulations but not a preferred term)
LOTE	Languages other than English
LTEL/LTELL	Long-term English (language) learner
SIFE/SLIFE	Students with (limited or) interrupted formal education

Educational reforms in the United States over the past two decades have increased the academic rigor of instruction and set forth accountability measures that negatively impact learners of English as a new language. English learners must do double the work in school by learning academic English at the same time that they study the core content areas of mathematics, science, history, English language arts, and other subjects. They are not given time to develop their English skills to intermediate or advanced levels of proficiency before they must participate in high-stakes assessments. They often take subject-area tests that have been designed and normed on native English speakers and, except in a few states, conducted in English. These tests are not valid or reliable for English learners (Abedi & Linquanti, 2007). Not surprisingly, the achievement gap between English learners and non-English learners has not narrowed in the past fifteen years (Murphy, 2014; U.S. Department of Education, n.d.). The long-term effects of the achievement gap include significantly higher dropout rates among English learners when compared with non-English learners, as found in studies in states like California (Rumberger, 2011).

Changes in the educational landscape may have repercussions for English language learning programs. In some instances, when schools and districts have not performed well on state tests, the English learners have been held responsible, along with other subgroups of learners, such as special education students. When policymakers and the general public do not understand the second language acquisition process and do not realize that the teaching staff may not have the educational background or experience to work well with students new to English, they falsely blame the learners and their families. Sometimes the poor performance on state tests gives rise to additional funds and other supports, but other times schools are taken over or closed down, staff leave or are shifted elsewhere, and low expectations for the students grow more widespread (Smyth, 2008; Sunderman, Kim, & Orfield, 2005).

Anti-immigrant bias in the United States has been more overt in recent years, and this circumstance has implications for our learners and programs. Even though more than 70 percent of the English learners in our pre-K–12 schools were born in the United States (Zong & Batalova, 2015), public rhetoric often equates "English learner" with "immigrant," and, sometimes, "undocumented immigrant," at that. If some people see English language development programs as a drain on school resources or believe that we should not educate "those people," our legal and moral obligations to provide the best education possible to all students can be upended. School budgets may not pass, internships and specialized courses for high schoolers may not be offered, and teacher inservice training may not be funded.

Educators in the United States have requested guidance regarding best practices for English learners in the current educational and sociopolitical environment. TESOL is the leading organization of language teaching professionals in the United States, and its mission is to advance the quality of English language teaching through professional development, research, standards, and advocacy. In 1997, TESOL released the first-ever pre-K–12 standards for English as a second language, and its commitment to helping educators implement those standards and others produced subsequently is unwavering (TESOL, 1997, 2006). In this era of rigorous standards and high-stakes testing, TESOL is well positioned to guide educators by focusing not on what language standards are, but on the "why," "what," and "how" of high-quality teaching. The stakes are high. Students are expected to become college- and career-ready, and that means they will need advanced levels of proficiency in English and the content area knowledge expected of high school graduates.

TESOL's Vision for Exemplary Teaching of English Learners

The conviction that knowing more than one language and culture benefits all students is a core value that was promulgated in TESOL's first ESL standards document in 1997 and has been included in other standards and position papers over time. It remains a hallmark of TESOL's vision today. The world is an interconnected place, and we all engage with linguistically and culturally diverse people. Technologies and trade have brought us closer together and require cross-cultural communication. Effective education in the 21st century calls for schools to provide opportunities for all students—not just English learners—to learn about other cultures and to learn world languages (Commission on Language Learning, 2017). Knowing more than one language has individual and societal benefits, and diversity typically fosters creativity (Keysar, Hayakawa, & An, 2011; Marian & Shook, 2013). Understanding different perspectives, life experiences, and world views enriches us and builds intercultural competence (TESOL, 1997).

In TESOL's vision, English learners can be successful in school and beyond. In our schools, English learners can share their viewpoints with English-speaking peers, teachers, administrators, and other members of the school community, who in turn can share theirs with the English learners. Learners can achieve advanced levels of English proficiency, thrive in English-medium content-area courses, become language-ready for universities, careers, or other personal goals, and maintain their native language and culture while adding English. We heartily believe that these targets can be reached in effective English language programs that demonstrate the following characteristics:

Curricula for English learners are rigorous, relevant, and designed and delivered with second language learning in mind. For many years—indeed, for most of the 20th century—English learners in the United States were relegated to language development classes, with few opportunities to receive grade-level content instruction until they reached advanced levels of proficiency. When educational practices changed, particularly in the 1990s, English learners were often on the receiving end of watered-down curricula and lower expectations than those that educators held for non-English learners. That situation should not be the case today. The standards and curricula for our learners need to be rigorous and relevant to their educational goals. Instructional practices such as the use of scaffolds, extended time, native language supports, and other aspects of differentiation help students gain access to the curricula and accommodate their proficiency levels. At times, specialized courses may be needed for students with interrupted or limited educational backgrounds. Overall, however, we need to have not only high expectations for our students but also targeted professional development for our teachers so that they can best serve their English learners as they progress through the second language acquisition process (California Department of Education, 2010; Cloud, Genesee, & Hamayan, 2009; U.S. Department of Education & U.S. Department of Justice [USED & USDOJ], 2015).

English learners, including learners with special needs, have access to all programs and services. In the United States, English learners must have access to English language development (ELD) services and grade-level content. School districts have a legal obligation to ensure that these learners can participate meaningfully and equally in educational programs and services (USED & USDOJ, 2015). The programs that are offered to English learners must meet a three-pronged legal test: the programs must (1) be based on sound education theory and principles, (2) be implemented with adequate personnel and resources and appropriate instructional practices, and (3) demonstrate that language barriers are being overcome within a reasonable period of time so that English learners attain parity with English-speaking class-mates in instructional programs (*Castañeda v. Pickard*, 1981). Furthermore, English learners who are dually identified with a learning disability must receive both ELD and special education services, and language proficiency should not be a factor in determining eligibility for gifted and talented programs (Burr, Haas, & Ferriere, 2015).

All educational personnel assume responsibility for the education of English learners. Helping English learners succeed in school must be the job of all teachers—not solely the ESL or bilingual ones. Academic language as used in school settings to meet rigorous standards, curricula, and assessments is more challenging to learn than social language, (as detailed in Chapter 2). English learners must develop literacy skills for each content area *in* their second language as they simultaneously learn, comprehend, and apply content-area concepts *through* their second language (Short & Echevarria, 2016). Indeed, English learners must do double the work in schools—learning English *and* learning content—but they are not given double the time (Short & Fitzsimmons, 2007). Apart from a one-year's grace period for language arts assessments, English learners are evaluated with the same tests as their English-speaking classmates, no matter what their English proficiency level is. The learners therefore need to maximize the time learning both academic English and content throughout the school day and that can happen only when all their teachers target both areas as lesson objectives and plan instruction accordingly (Ballantyne, Sanderman, & Levy, 2008; Echevarría, Vogt, & Short, 2017; Horwitz et al., 2009).

All educational personnel

- respect, affirm, and promote students' home languages and cultural knowledge and experiences as resources;
- celebrate multilingualism and diversity;
- support policies that promote individual language rights and multicultural education;
- help prepare students to be global citizens.

Our goal is for English learners to be successful wherever and whenever they use English. However, we also want them to have opportunities to maintain and further develop their own language and be part of a community that respects their cultures (Canagarajah & Wurr, 2011; García, Skutnabb-Kangas, & Torres-Guzmán, 2006). In many parts of the world, children learn a second and even a third language, sometimes at home, sometimes at school. This relatively normal practice of learning more than one language should be celebrated and encouraged. We know that being bilingual generates cognitive and societal benefits, and it is certainly valuable in many careers. We should never try to eliminate a student's home language or culture. Instead, teachers and administrators must welcome diversity in the schools, and they must be given the skills as part of their training to work with linguistically and culturally diverse learners and their families (Nieto & Bode, 2008).

TESOL professionals are recognized as specialists with accurate knowledge, skills, and dispositions for providing high-quality English language teaching. Our profession has struggled over the years with the false notion that if you speak English, you can teach English. Becoming an effective teacher of English learners is not equivalent to having native-speaking skills. TESOL professionals study a range of courses or topics such as second language acquisition theory, ESL and sheltered instruction methods, and teaching reading to non-native speakers of

English. They know how language works as a system, how to plan and differentiate instruction for English learners and others who struggle with academic literacy in language arts and content courses, how culture affects learning and communication, how to assess students with low levels of English literacy, and how to interpret and apply results of language assessments. They typically have a practicum where they work in schools with English learners while getting their degree. They stay up-to-date with research and policy once they are practicing teachers (see López, Scanlan, & Gundrum, 2013; National Board for Professional Teaching Standards, 2010; TESOL International Association, 2013, 2018). In many U.S. K–12 public schools, the second language teachers must have either an ESL/ELD or bilingual teaching certificate or license or an elementary or content area teaching certificate or license with an ESL endorsement. In a number of states, they must pass a professional exam as well.

TESOL professionals are valued by colleagues and other educators for their expertise and consulted in instructional, programming, and policy decision-making. Because of their knowledge in the fields of second language learning, ESL methodology, and cross-cultural communication, ESL/ELD, bilingual, and dual language teachers are valuable resources for colleagues and administrators in schools and districts. Through collaborative endeavors such as professional learning groups, school improvement teams, textbook selection committees, and the like, their expertise is tapped as a resource for providing the best possible programming, instruction, and materials for English learners. TESOL professionals can help colleagues adjust their teaching and testing practices according to the proficiency levels of the students in class and can design interventions for newcomers and long-term English learners. They can advise fellow teachers and administrators about the students' cultures and support them in communicating with parents (Cambridge English Teaching Framework, 2015; TESOL International Association, 2013, 2018; Valdés, Kibler, & Walqui, 2014).

Policies, programs, and practices are based on current research and accurate information. It is critical for policymakers and administrators to rely on research as they establish policies, develop or refine programs, and promote instructional and assessment practices. (See Appendix A for a description of the most common programs for English learners in the United States.) Building a program around anecdotes and myths will not result in student success. Students do not learn to speak academic English well just by being exposed to it. In the past, children did not learn English easily and rapidly. Because a child speaks English does not mean she or he is proficient in all four language domains at an advanced academic level. Over the past thirty years, research has become more rigorous, and we know more about how a second language is learned. It takes time and investments in resources. Skimping on these will not yield the educational or economic outcomes that schools seek and society needs (California Department of Education, 2010; Horwitz et al., 2009).

The 6 Principles for Exemplary Teaching of English Learners

The 6 Principles put forth in this book are not revolutionary or groundbreaking concepts in language learning. They are well-established guidelines drawn from decades of research in language pedagogy and language acquisition theory. We present them in seemingly simple statements, yet they carry substantial weight because how well they are implemented can make the difference between student success and struggle. The 6 Principles must be taken together, as a cohesive whole. One cannot just know one's learners, for example, and then not act on that knowledge when planning instruction.

Figure 1.1 provides a brief explanation of each principle, and later chapters show educators of English learners how the 6 Principles may be realized in and out of the classroom.

FIGURE 1.1	The 6 Principles for Exemplary Teaching of English Learners

Exemplary teaching of English learners rests on the following 6 Principles:

1. **Know your learners.** Teachers learn basic information about their students' families, languages, cultures, and educational backgrounds to engage them in the classrooms and prepare and deliver lessons more effectively.

2. **Create conditions for language learning.** Teachers create a classroom culture that will ensure that students feel comfortable in the class. They make decisions regarding the physical environment, the materials, and the social integration of students to promote language learning.

3. **Design high-quality lessons for language development.** Teachers plan meaningful lessons that promote language learning and help students develop learning strategies and critical thinking skills. These lessons evolve from the learning objectives.

4. **Adapt lesson delivery as needed.** Teachers continually assess as they teach—observing and reflecting on learners' responses to determine whether the students are reaching the learning objectives. If students struggle or are not challenged enough, teachers consider the possible reasons and adjust their lessons.

5. **Monitor and assess student language development.** Language learners learn at different rates, so teachers regularly monitor and assess their language development in order to advance their learning efficiently. Teachers also gather data to measure student language growth.

6. **Engage and collaborate within a community of practice.** Teachers collaborate with others in the profession to provide the best support for their learners with respect to programming, instruction, and advocacy. They also continue their own professional learning.

A Look Back and a Look Ahead

More and more people are learning English every day. It is critically important that their teachers make informed decisions about their instructional and assessment practices. This book supports teachers in this work.

In this chapter, we have

- explained TESOL's rationale for identifying core principles for exemplary teaching of English learners and the pressing need for their implementation in K–12 classrooms in the United States;

- shared TESOL's vision of effective education, which includes honoring home languages and cultures, recognizing TESOL professionals as specialists in language education, and ensuring that English learners have access to challenging, rigorous curricula; and

- introduced the 6 Principles, which are discussed in detail in Chapter 3. These principles help teachers create conditions in the classroom that promote language learning and plan and deliver lessons that keep learners' needs, interests, and backgrounds in mind.

Teachers of English learners need to understand that language development is dynamic and not always linear and that how well we communicate is measured by our purpose and audience. One aspect of making choices related to language teaching methods and techniques is knowing how second languages are learned and what inhibits or facilitates the learning process. Chapter 2 explores what academic language is in schools, how students' levels of language proficiency influences their performance of tasks in English, and various factors that support learning English as a new language. The goal is that when teachers apply the 6 Principles in their classrooms, they will do so knowledgably and with their learners' needs in mind.

Additional resources pertaining to this chapter are available at www.the6principles.org/K-12.

2 WHAT TEACHERS SHOULD KNOW ABOUT ENGLISH LANGUAGE DEVELOPMENT TO PLAN INSTRUCTION

The 6 Principles are not new concepts. Rather, they build on the findings of several decades of research on second language acquisition and English language teaching. They are consistent with the recommendations found in several syntheses of research on educating language minority students in U.S. schools (August & Shanahan, 2006; Baker et al., 2014; National Academies of Sciences, Engineering, and Medicine [NASEM], 2017). More importantly, they represent an assets-based approach, which views English learners' home languages and cultures as resources to draw on and make a valuable part of the classroom for the benefit of all students.

Before we delve into the 6 Principles and their implementation in the classroom in Chapter 3, a brief discussion of the main concepts of second language and literacy development will be useful. We have all experienced learning our home language, although not all of us have learned a second or third language. In Chapter 2 we explore what it takes to learn a second language, what a natural progression through levels of proficiency might be, and what a vital role language plays in school.

Multiple times every day teachers make instructional decisions about how to convey information to English learners and how to determine whether they understand the material and are making progress in their language development. Yet most teachers do not think of themselves as language teachers. When asked, they identify themselves by saying *"I'm a math teacher"* or *"I teach social studies."* In these responses, they imply that their content expertise frames their teaching responsibilities and that teaching language to students is not their task.

Every teacher, though, relies on language as a tool—a tool to develop students' content knowledge. They explain, lead discussions, assign readings, and expect students to complete written assessments. Each of these teaching tasks entails as much knowledge of language as knowledge of the content. And so, every teacher who relies on language as an instructional tool is a language teacher. We want to encourage every teacher to recognize this fact, take ownership of this role, and design their lessons with language learning in mind.

Knowing how the language acquisition process works can help teachers with their instructional decisions, both in their planning of a lesson and in their delivery of it. If a learner makes an error in English, for example, a teacher's response should be based on whether the error is normal for a given proficiency level or whether it indicates something that has been learned incorrectly or not at all. Not only are effective teachers of English learners conscious of their role as language teachers, but they are also willing and intentional about it. They have reasonable expectations for learners because they are aware of the time, effort, and practice that it takes to learn a new language.

So, in this chapter, we provide foundational knowledge for language teaching. First, we look specifically at how academic language can develop in school. As teachers, we need to know our students' proficiency levels in academic English in order to design appropriate instruction and have reasonable expectations for what they can do and what they need to reach the next level. Next, we examine some essential and beneficial conditions for language learning and additional factors that may help or hinder progress. When teachers know which of these they have some control over, they can boost language learning. For example, when teachers know that language develops through use and interaction, they can plan lessons that encourage students to use language actively and to draw on their home language as a resource. Finally, we explain the important connection between language and identity. Language use reflects identity and teachers can play an important role in helping learners see themselves as competent bilinguals or multilinguals.

Developing Academic Language Proficiency

To develop English learners' proficiency with academic language, teachers need to understand the role of language in school. They must consider the differences between social and academic language, as well as the characteristics of academic English. They need to take account of standards that define English language proficiency for different contexts and purposes. In monitoring their students' progress toward proficiency, teachers also need to consider research-based levels of language development and reasonable time frames for their students to achieve proficiency.

The Role of Language in School

This is my puppet friend, Mister Green. He has a big mouth, doesn't he? Mister Green loves to eat big numbers. Big numbers are yummy, aren't they, Mister Green? If I have the number 15 and the number 12, and if Mister Green loves big numbers, who can tell me which number he would eat?

(Second grade math)

Roberto, come on up here. Here is your patch of dirt, right here on the floor. I want you to stand in your patch of dirt here, and you are going to be a plant. You are going to be a plant and you are going to grow. He is a nice, happy plant, wouldn't you say? Plants grow if they are feeling happy, and they make seeds. But what happens if the plant grows too big for its small place, and it gets very crowded where the big plant is? Can the big plant just walk away to some place with more dirt?

(Second grade science)

Record 15 minutes of your own teaching, observe a class, or watch a classroom video. Note how you (or the teacher) and students rely on language to communicate meaning. What is the teacher saying, word for word? What language are the students hearing and producing orally and/or in writing? In addition to language, in what other ways is meaning being conveyed? Reflect on the role of language in the instructional segment.

Effective teaching of English learners in the classroom begins with an understanding of the role of the English language in instruction. Teachers who grew up and were educated themselves in a classroom where all students spoke English proficiently may overlook the prominent role of language in their lessons. Like the teachers in the vignettes above, they may hold an expectation that every student will be able to follow teacher talk, ask questions, answer in intelligible speech, and participate in classroom discussions. Likewise, they may have an expectation of shared cultural experiences and a common ground of beliefs and assumptions. With English learners in the classroom, however, teachers can feel at a loss when they realize how much they rely on English to teach.

Effective teachers recognize that teaching linguistically diverse students is a three-part challenge (see figure 2.1):

1. They must depart from the predominantly language-based instruction and use a full repertoire of resources for meaning-making. These include pictorial, gestural, experiential, interactional, and linguistic supports.

2. They need ways in which they can help the students draw on their own available resources, such as linguistic, social, experiential, cognitive, and strategic knowledge.

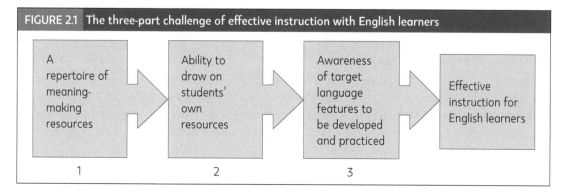

FIGURE 2.1 The three-part challenge of effective instruction with English learners

A repertoire of meaning-making resources	Ability to draw on students' own resources	Awareness of target language features to be developed and practiced	Effective instruction for English learners
1	2	3	

3. They must become aware of the target language features that students need to develop to be fully functional in the classroom and with the specific content they are learning. They also need approaches to explicitly teach these target language forms at the same time that they are teaching their content. (See a brief video on the three-part challenge at www.the6principles.org/K-12.)

When we observe students' language use in different grades, we see that all students become more proficient with language over time. Effective teachers adjust to this development and match their own language use to the linguistic abilities of their students. A kindergarten teacher speaks differently from a third-grade or a sixth-grade teacher. The following classroom vignettes illustrate this.

Point the flashlight on the word "like." Good. Give the light to Amanda. Amanda will point to the word "and." Good. Give it to Sophia. She is going to point to the word "go." Very good. Give it to Victoria. She is going to point to the word "will."

(Kindergarten teacher, Ms. Mullet)

We are learning today about the main idea of the story and how to find the supporting details. But you know how I am. I don't only want you to find the supporting details. I want you to tell me why they are the supporting details. Olivia, what is a supporting detail?

(Third-grade teacher, Mrs. Willis)

As we are reading today, if you feel that you want to underline or annotate the text to help you better understand, please go ahead and do that at any time. If you want to underline evidence to cite in your answer, do that because that's what good readers do.

(Sixth-grade teacher, Mr. Willoughby)

All three teachers use language appropriate for the grade level. Notice that the kindergarten teacher, Ms. Mullet, uses short, familiar utterance frames, which she keeps repeating with just minor variations so that students can focus on the task and not struggle with her instructions. She uses only words that are among the most frequent in the English language and that young children who have a vocabulary of a few thousand words will know.

The utterances of the third-grade teacher, Mrs. Willis, are longer, but she still starts them with the basic subjects (*we, you, I*) and uses only two less common, technical terms (*main idea, supporting detail*). She repeats the key term, *supporting detail*, and immediately invites a student to explain it.

When addressing sixth graders, Mr. Willoughby speaks in long sentences that do not start with the subject. Not only are his utterances syntactically complex but they also begin with dependent clauses, making them much more challenging to comprehend. In addition, Mr. Willoughby includes four technical terms (*underline, annotate, evidence, cite*).

Constantly monitoring students' understanding and using instructional language to match their English language proficiency are hallmarks of high-quality teacher communication. Many teachers do this routinely when they instruct native English speakers in different grades; however, with English learners, they need to be able to make adjustments even more skillfully, much as they would when teaching in a different grade. Teachers need to be mindful of target language features and steer students toward noticing, practicing, and using these features frequently in the classroom.

Social and Academic Language

Students who are learning English through informal communication tend to master social language first, much sooner than they are able to communicate in formal ways. Social language is conversational and requires mainly listening and speaking, a vocabulary of a few thousand words, and the mastery of frequently heard utterance patterns. Students' mastery of social language does not indicate proficiency in academic language. In contrast, students who learned English in foreign countries through grammar drills and academic reading are not likely to have acquired proficiency in social language. Of the two types, social and academic, formal academic language is the more challenging to learn and is what is needed in school.

The distinction between social and academic, or informal and formal, language is not binary. First, different skills are involved. Social language is conducted primarily through listening and speaking, whereas academic language also requires a large amount of reading and writing. Second, development from social to academic language unfolds along a continuum, with elements mastered gradually, over years of practice.

The Continuum from Social to Academic Language

Three students and their teacher are describing the same photograph in a language arts textbook.

More Social

FELIPE: Here, two people at an old building. She's up there. She's looking down. He's looking up. He's saying something—like, "Girl, you're great. I like you. Can you come down?"

ZHIHUI: I see a picture that's in black-and-white. I see a building and a balcony. I also see the sun shining in, which means that it's the morning. I see Romeo looking up at Juliet, and Juliet looking down at Romeo.

BARIKA: This is a scene from the play *Romeo and Juliet*. I see a backdrop with a sky. The female lead role is Juliet, who is standing on the balcony of a palace. The balcony and the wall look antique. The picture has a dramatic feeling.

TEACHER: This is a black-and-white photograph of a theater stage. It captures the famous balcony scene of the play *Romeo and Juliet*. The stage set shows the classical architecture of a weathered palace at dawn. The breaking light casts shadows on the main characters. Although Juliet is on the balcony and Romeo is on the ground, their eyes are locked as they are absorbed in their conversation.

More Academic

Characteristics of Academic English

Academic language is important for anyone studying content through English or planning a professional career that uses English. It is integral to a student's academic success within the type of standards-based curricula found in U.S. schools and is the core of TESOL's pre-K–12 English language proficiency standards (TESOL, 2006). (See www.tesol.org/advance-the-field/standards for more information.) Academic language is the language of textbooks, informational texts, scholarly papers, instructional videos, academic presentations, and lectures. Table 2.1 displays the main characteristics of academic language, at the conceptual, discourse, sentence, and word levels. To be considered proficient, English learners need to approach the academic language skills of their grade-level peers.

Table 2.1	Characteristics of proficient academic English	
Characteristic	Explanation of characteristic	Examples
Conceptual level		
Conceptual complexity	The treatment reflects cognitive functions: describing, explaining, comparing, classifying, sequencing, justifying, analyzing, evaluating, synthesizing.	*This is what it looks like . . .* *This belongs in the category of . . .* *This is an important choice because . . .* *These phenomena are related in this way.*
Development	Adequate details are provided. Claims are supported.	*This means that . . . For example, . . .* *The sources of this information are . . .*
Abstraction	Concrete events and objects are treated as representations of abstract concepts.	*Expertise is a key aspect of professional identity.*
Figurativeness	Abstract terms are assigned attributes of concrete things or live beings: they can move, communicate, or have intentions.	*A solution surfaced.* *The position commands respect.* *The analysis was deceiving.*
Detachment	The speaker/writer separates from the message to suggest objectivity and logical reasoning.	*Research shows that . . .* *The evidence points to . . .*
Discourse level		
Organization	Ideas follow a logical progression. The topics are controlled. The connections between ideas are marked.	*First, . . . Second, . . . Then, . . . Finally, . . .* *Nevertheless, consequently, likewise*
Cohesion	Words and sentences are linked. Key words are repeated strategically. Pronouns match their referents.	*<u>Visual representations</u> can help us solve math problems. <u>For example</u>, a number line is one form of <u>visual representation</u>. It can show . . .*
Conciseness	Information is densely packed. Meanings are nuanced.	*Currently, the annual mean growth rate of carbon dioxide in the Earth's atmosphere is 2.1 parts per million.*
Genre	The conventions of different genres are observed.	Opinion essay, news article, journal article, interview, technical report
Sentence level		
Precision	Sentences are complete, and each is formed with care. Qualifiers are frequent.	*It is <u>mostly</u> true. Results <u>could</u> improve.* *The best solution <u>may</u> be . . .*
Syntactic complexity	Phrase and sentence structures are varied and developed. Sentences are long.	*When we are working more than ever before to be able to afford the purchases we are choosing to make, we are spending less time with the people who make our lives happy.*
Density	Information is packed into elaborate noun phrases.	*<u>Several justifiable grievances against the released draft of the proposed health care law</u> were raised.*

(continued on the next page)

Table 2.1	Characteristics of proficient academic English *(continued)*	
Characteristic	Explanation of characteristic	Examples
Sentence level (continued)		
Grammar	Sentences adhere to the rules of formal grammar. Grammatical features that are less common in social language appear often (passive voice, embedded clauses, modal auxiliaries, range in verb tense and aspect).	*Lawmakers were given . . .* *Feedback should have been considered.* *Had there been more discussion, . . .*
Mechanics	Error-free spelling and accurate punctuation	
Word level		
Exactness	Words are intentionally selected from a set of vocabulary alternatives with regard to their frequency, connotations, and suitable collocates.	Alternatives for *"go down": happiness decreases; the price drops; the plane descends; stocks plummet*
Conciseness	Ideas are condensed into technical terms. Extra words are omitted to avoid wordiness.	*climate agreement, protagonist, absolute value, parallelism* *Due to the fact that vs. because* *In the event that vs. if*
Variety	Word repetition is avoided except for key words and for effect.	
Clarity	The pronunciation of words reflects knowledge of sound patterns and word stress.	*The Whíte House v. a white hóuse* *bénefit, benefícial, beneficíary*

(Anstrom et al., 2010; Short & Echevarría, 2016; WIDA, 2012; Zwiers, 2014)

Standards for English Language Proficiency

Who Is an English Learner?

Is the student an English learner?

"I don't think so. Mom speaks English."

"He shouldn't be. We can understand each other without any trouble."

"No, he was born in the U.S."

"We don't know. She has never been tested for English language proficiency."

"Of course. Her first language is Mandarin, and she rarely speaks in class."

"He must be. He speaks English with a strong accent."

English language specialists frequently hear unsound explanations like these from teachers when they inquire about specific students. Statements like these reflect the fact that many teachers tend to rely on their own casual interpretation of what it means to be an English learner. However, English language specialists go by a more formal definition, one defined by law. This definition does not equate English learner status with being born outside the United States, or having a home language other than English, or speaking with an obvious accent. Rather, the formal meaning of the term is that the student has not yet reached the level of English language proficiency that the state has defined as sufficient to succeed academically in the curriculum.

Most English learners in K–12 settings were born in the United States. Neither speaking with an accent nor being silent in class is a reliable indicator of English learner status. Often parents and children are proficient in several languages, and sometimes the current caregivers are not the persons who have raised the student. Teachers should consult their district's identification and exit criteria as well as their students' English language proficiency scores to know with certainty which students have the temporary designation of English learner.

Although children can acquire the basic social language that they need by actively engaging in communication, this form of language acquisition is insufficient for the vast majority of English learners in school. The task of acquiring a new language to the degree that one needs to succeed academically or professionally in that language is surprisingly lengthy and complex. Fully appreciating the complexity of this undertaking is difficult for anyone who has not tried to learn a new language.

Various language proficiency standards exist to define language proficiency for different contexts and different purposes around the world (see, for example, Council of Europe, 2011). In the United States, English language proficiency for K–12 learners is guided by federal law (Every Student Succeeds Act [ESSA], 2015, Sec. 1111 [b][1][F]). The law requires each state to have English language proficiency standards defined for the domains of listening, speaking, reading, and writing. The standards should address different proficiency levels and align with each state's academic standards. The purpose of these standards is to ensure that English learners "attain English proficiency and develop high levels of academic achievement in English" and that "all English learners can meet the same challenging State academic standards that all children are expected to meet" (ESSA, 2015, Sec. 3102 [1–2]). Practically speaking, this means that English learners must develop functional, grade-level use of English so they can be successful academically in content courses that follow state standards. Each state must choose (1) the English language proficiency standards that best serve as a benchmark for its learning standards in the content areas and (2) the proficiency test that assesses the extent to which each student has attained them.

It is important for teachers to recognize that English language proficiency in the U.S. K–12 context is a tool for moving students toward meaningful participation in grade-level instruction and not an exclusive educational goal. Nor is the goal for learners to be indistinguishable from monolingual speakers of English. Nor is it for them simply to blend in within the English-speaking classroom. The standards of English language proficiency for U.S. schools focus on what students can do with language in content-based instruction.

TESOL International Association adopted English language proficiency standards for pre-K–12 learners (TESOL, 2006) that are related to the widely-used standards of the WIDA Consortium states (WIDA, 2012).[1] These standards set a long-term goal for English learners to demonstrate mastery of language use in five domains: (1) social and instructional language, (2) the language of language arts, (3) the language of mathematics, (4) the language of science, and (5) the language of social studies. Each of the five domains includes proficiency in four modalities: listening, speaking, reading, and writing.

TESOL Pre-K–12 English Language Proficiency Standards (TESOL, 2006)

Standard 1: English language learners communicate for social, intercultural, and instructional purposes within the school setting.

Standard 2: English language learners communicate information, ideas, and concepts necessary for academic success in the area of language arts.

Standard 3: English language learners communicate information, ideas, and concepts necessary for academic success in the area of mathematics.

Standard 4: English language learners communicate information, ideas, and concepts necessary for academic success in the area of science.

Standard 5: English language learners communicate information, ideas, and concepts necessary for academic success in the area of social studies.

---

[1] More than 35 states compose the WIDA Consortium. Other states, such as California, Texas, and New York, have their own standards that similarly call for students to develop academic English.

Levels of English Language Development

The development of language is not unlike the physical growth of children; it is continuous, incremental, and unnoticed except during or following periodic growth spurts. Children who are developing in a healthy manner—interacting with other speakers and employing language frequently for a variety of purposes—develop new language gradually. Each day they can comprehend and produce more words, add to their stock of language formulas, and surprise us with their utterances and increasingly sophisticated phrases. They can communicate meaning about a greater variety of topics, in more nuanced ways. In short, language is not an all-or-nothing ability but a lengthy developmental trajectory, which can be advanced or thwarted depending on conditions, of which the most significant ones are deliberate practice through frequent use, motivation to communicate, the availability of comprehensible input, and usable feedback. (See a brief video on proficiency in a new language at www.the6principles.org/K-12.)

For the purposes of instruction and assessment, experts have divided language development into levels and have described what language use typically looks like or sounds like at every level for each of the four language skills (listening, speaking, reading, and writing). In the United States, most states identify five levels of English proficiency with a sixth level that represents grade-level language functionality. These levels should guide teachers in their observations of students and their instructional planning (Dutro & Kinsella, 2010; Gottlieb, Katz, & Ernst-Slavit, 2009; Fairbairn & Jones-Vo, 2010; Nutta et al., 2014; WIDA, 2012).

However, it is important to realize that language development is not inevitable along those trajectories, or steady, or balanced across the four language skill areas. Students may, for example, progress faster in speaking than they do in writing. And, of course, much of language development is latent, takes place in the mind, and is often difficult to characterize in terms of observable language use. With careful attention, teachers can learn to recognize the markers that indicate language development:

- Increased length of utterances (oral or written phrases and sentences)
- Greater variety of utterance patterns
- Broader choice of words and greater awareness of their appropriateness to convey intended meaning
- Increased comprehensibility of the ideas being communicated
- Increased appropriateness of the level of formality (register) to audience and occasion
- Decreased use of hesitation phenomena (*ah, hm, er*)
- Reduced use of filler expressions (*stuff like that, you know*) and formulaic phrases

---

Collect several samples of an English learner's oral or written language. If possible, compare different samples that are months apart. Evaluate the changes that you recognize by looking carefully for the markers of language development:

1. An increase in the mean length of utterances (MLU)
2. A greater variety in the types of phrases and utterances
3. A broader choice of words
4. An increase in the comprehensibility of what is being communicated
5. A reduction in formulaic phrases, patterned language, hesitation sounds, and filler expressions
6. A broader choice of register (degree of formality)

Students who rely on sentence fragments, repetitive structures, and formulaic expressions are usually less proficient than those who produce a lot of detail and variety in their language, who choose their words carefully, and who can change the way in which they express themselves, depending on the conversation partner or communicative situation.

The conditions for language acquisition vary for language learners, and students do not pass through these proficiency levels in an identical manner. Some learners show evidence of language gains in bursts, whereas others plateau, especially in the absence of regular interaction with proficient speakers and beneficial feedback. The levels indicate a hypothesized progression to functional grade-level English language proficiency at the end of about six years. This is a rigorous expectation for English learners, who are acquiring the language at the same time that they are learning grade-level content in English.

The markers of language development shown on the previous page are embedded in the three components that characterize English language proficiency at each level: utterance variety and control, vocabulary use, and communicative functions and registers (WIDA, 2012). Descriptions of these components follow:

- **Utterance variety and control.** One aspect of language development is the ability to form phrases and sentences with varying complexity. Learners usually begin with memorized chunks (*I got it*, *that's easy*, *what's this*) and progress to one- or two-word responses and simple phrases (*this part*, *the red one*, *can't see*, *show me*, *I have it*). Over time, they develop a repertoire of common phrase structures (*in the picture/book*, *look at this/ that one*, *it's good/nice*, *read/do it with me*). They can combine these phrases into longer utterances: *I like to play soccer with my friends. I'm coloring the circle blue.* But they are still a long way from being able to control complex utterances like *When I color over the blue circle with a yellow crayon, I get a green circle*; *I found the answer by taking away 2 from 14, which is 12*; or *If I had a garden, I would plant all kinds of fruit trees*.

  Utterance control involves being able to make a great number of grammatical changes as needed. These might include, for example, forming the plural of nouns; using articles, prepositions, and pronouns appropriately; changing verb tenses and using modal auxiliaries; forming questions and negative statements; and making subjects and verbs agree. Developing this control requires attention to these forms and abundant opportunities for practice and use until these skills are firmly established.

- **Vocabulary use.** Another main component of language development is the growth of word knowledge, in breadth, depth, and accuracy. Vocabulary learning begins with learning labels for concrete objects, followed by using a small handful of modifying words that can cluster with those object names to express a more complete idea (for example, *car— blue car—car here—car go—my car*). Although learning the names of concrete objects is usually the easiest, the most important words to prioritize for teaching are those that are the most frequent across all types of uses. Among these are the function words that play a role in grammar (also known as "mortar words" because they hold content words together). These function words are auxiliaries (*be*, *do*, *have*), modal auxiliaries (*can*, *may*, *should*), prepositions (*in*, *with*), pronouns (*it*, *they*, *that*), articles (*a*, *the*), determiners (*some*, *few*), conjunctions (*and*, *so*), and conjunctive adverbs (*consequently*, *finally*). These words help students connect ideas. Productive vocabulary knowledge also includes knowing word parts (prefixes, suffixes, and roots) as well as identifying cognates (words that are similar in spelling and/or pronunciation and have related meaning in one's native language).

  Word knowledge is incremental; with each new encounter, learners can add new details, associations, and multiple meanings to a word. The word is gradually networked into a semantic web in the learner's brain. Depth of word knowledge also entails knowing which words occur together to form expected collocations. For example, in English we say *do homework*, not *make the homework*. We *share our thoughts* but we do not *divide our thoughts*. We eat *fast food* but not *slow food*.

The most challenging aspect of vocabulary use is fixed expressions and idioms, which require memorization of multiword units with opaque meanings—that is, they cannot be easily interpreted from their parts. Fixed expressions may be easier than idioms in that many are ubiquitous (*What was that again? To be perfectly honest with you; Actually, the thing about it is that*). Idioms, by contrast, are the ultimate challenge; they are opaque, rarely taught to language learners, and make sense only if produced exactly word-for-word (*Cat got your tongue? Turn the other cheek*).

The Types of Words to Learn

- **High frequency words.** The 2,800 most-frequent word families cover 90 percent of all that is spoken and written in English. A current source for this vocabulary is the New General Service List (www.newgeneralservicelist.org).
- **Sight words.** These are the most-frequent written words, which every learner should recognize automatically—without sounding them out—to build speed and fluency in reading.
- **General academic words.** Some academic vocabulary is less subject-specific. These terms are cross-curricular and thus useful in every discipline. A current source is the New Academic Word List (www.newacademicwordlist.org/), which contains 960 headwords.
- **Content vocabulary commonly used in the elementary grades.** These terms are specific to a content area and to the grade level. A notable collection is *Words Worth Teaching* (Biemiller, 2010), which focuses on the meanings known by children in K–2 and 3–6. In addition, some districts have developed their own curricular content word lists by grade and by subject.

- **Communicative functions and registers.** The third component of language proficiency is the ability to accomplish specific communicative functions and tasks by using written and spoken language. Many of these functions—or purposes for using language, such as to disagree or to describe—can be achieved with varying degrees of formality—in other words, by using different registers. Consider, for example, the communicative function of asking someone for clarification. To achieve this, one might say *Huh? What's that?* or *I'm sorry, would you mind repeating that more slowly?* A proficient speaker is cognizant of the varieties of language use and can adjust the register (the formality of the language) to fit a specific social situation.

Teachers need to focus on these three components of language development as they work with English learners, and they must keep in mind the time that students have had to learn English. Figure 2.2 illustrates how the three components expand over time as learners progress through the levels and advance toward proficiency. Note that the number of proficiency levels is six, the most common organization in the United States. In the graphic, the narrow tip of the triangle represents the skills that novice language learners have, and the wide base of the triangle represents the skills that highly proficient learners demonstrate. The narrowness near the top suggests why students make faster progress through the lower proficiency levels—there is less to master—than they do with more advanced levels of proficiency. The features of the triangle—in particular, its substantial height and its expanding width toward the base—also suggest why it is so important for all teachers to pay attention to academic English in the content areas so they can specifically target instruction in those language skills and advance students' language learning.

Table 2.2 complements the graphic representation in figure 2.2 by summarizing the growth that occurs in utterance variety and control, vocabulary use, and communicative functions and

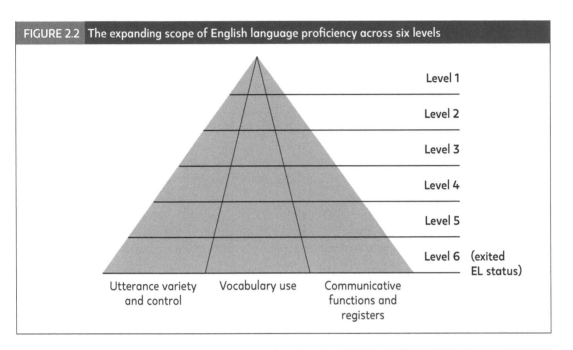

FIGURE 2.2 The expanding scope of English language proficiency across six levels

Level 1
Level 2
Level 3
Level 4
Level 5
Level 6 (exited EL status)

Utterance variety and control   Vocabulary use   Communicative functions and registers

Table 2.2	English language development levels		
	Utterance variety and control	Vocabulary use	Communicative functions and registers
Level 1	Relies on memorized phrases	Uses a small vocabulary of high-frequency words	Engages in a few types of familiar exchanges; requires native language or nonverbal supports for academic tasks
Level 2	Produces a variety of memorized phrases and a limited range of sentence patterns	Uses mostly high-frequency words and some content words	Participates in very simple verbal and written interactions; performs academic tasks with native language or other supports
Level 3	Forms a range of phrase and sentence patterns	Uses high and mid-frequency words, plus a few hundred content words	Interacts in most everyday situations, conveys information and asks questions; performs academic tasks with modifications
Level 4	Forms a wider range of utterance patterns with growing accuracy	Uses mid-frequency words as well as hundreds of technical and content words and some idioms	Participates in social interaction; expresses meaning in multiple, related sentences; distinguishes formal and informal registers; performs many academic tasks
Level 5	Forms a variety of utterance patterns into connected discourse with growing accuracy	Uses several thousand technical and content words as well as frequently used idioms and fixed expressions	Participates in extended discourse; switches purposefully between informal and formal registers; performs a wide range of communicative functions and academic tasks
Level 6 (Exited EL status, at grade-level language ability)	Fluently produces grade-level utterance patterns with accuracy	Uses grade-level vocabulary, including a variety of idioms and fixed expressions	Performs grade-level communicative functions, using informal and formal registers appropriately; performs academic tasks independently

registers as learners progress from level 1 to level 6 of English proficiency. The descriptions of language development at each level can help teachers identify learners' current level and chart their progress toward proficiency.

The Time Frame for Reaching Proficiency

We do not yet know definitively how long it takes to achieve English language proficiency in U.S. schools (NASEM, 2017). Research is growing, but the length of time depends on the assessment and achievement benchmarks used to define English language proficiency, and these vary by state, and even by year. The time also depends on the populations of learners, their grade of school entry, their initial English proficiency, the language support program they are enrolled in, and whether they have a learning disability.

The majority of identified English learners are born in the United States, and they start kindergarten or grade 1 with varying knowledge of English. Longitudinal research conducted in seven districts in the state of Washington with high percentages of English learners, high levels of poverty, and low academic achievement has shown that the average number of years for kindergartners to achieve English proficiency and be reclassified as former ELs was between 3 and 4 years, although 10–15 percent of the learners were still not proficient after 8 years—mainly those with disabilities or those who entered school with low initial proficiency (Greenberg Motamedi, 2015). Those who started kindergarten with advanced English proficiency still took 2.5 years on average to achieve full proficiency (Greenberg Motamedi, 2015). Students who were eligible for special education services took nearly two years longer to become proficient, and the rate of full proficiency after 8 years for those learners was only 75 percent.

Greenberg Motamedi (2015) also found that English learners who started in grades 2–5 took longer to reach reclassification. They needed on average 4.2 years to reach proficiency, but almost 20 percent were not yet proficient after 8 years. Many of them spent as much time moving from beginner to advanced levels as they did moving from advanced to grade-level proficiency. In light of the ideas illustrated in figure 2.2, this result is not surprising. As students move up in proficiency level and in grades, they have more to learn.

In sum, acquiring proficiency in English, and, specifically, in academic English, is an involved, long-term enterprise, which takes years of instruction and deliberate practice—for most students more than 4 years. The work does not stop when students are able to use social language fluently. The goal is to reach advanced, grade-level proficiency within the standards that have been adopted in a given state; however, that does not mean that students study language only until they are proficient in English. English learners should also have content courses in their daily schedule. When planned well, the mix of language and content instruction facilitates their English language development. However, it is important to keep in mind that being an English learner is a temporary designation, whereas being a competent multilingual is a lifelong asset, worthy of every teacher's support.

Conditions for Second Language Learning

We would all like to know the best way to teach a second language to any learner. However, although an entire field of research—second language acquisition—is dedicated to examining this topic, we do not yet have a definitive answer. A dozen theories focus on the neurological, psychological, cognitive, and/or linguistic processes by which people learn languages other than their mother tongue. Yet these theories have not necessarily focused on ideal ways of teaching a particular variety of a particular language—in this case, academic English—in a particular context—in this instance, U.S. K–12 classrooms (Lightbown & Spada, 2014; VanPatten & Williams, 2014; Valdés, Kibler, & Walqui, 2014; Williams, Mercer, & Ryan, 2015).

Despite the range of theories, we have learned from decades of research findings that some conditions are essential and some conditions are beneficial for second language acquisition. Some individual variables play a role, too.

Essential Conditions

Essential conditions are those that must be present for second language acquisition to occur. Teachers can play a role in promoting some of these. Essential conditions include the following:

1. **Neurophysiological capacity.** Language is a complex neurophysiological function. It can be thought of as software that runs on the hardware of the brain (Anderson & Lightfoot, 2002). Second language acquisition is facilitated by the software of the first language. In other words, a learner's acquisition of his or her home language established neurophysiological processing that plays a key role in how he or she handles input in a new language. Normal first language development indicates that all is well with the learner's neurophysiology for acquiring additional languages. Given this, teachers should inquire about students' experiences with primary language development and view rich primary language development as a strong foundation for learning new languages (Baker, 2014; Kohnert, 2013).

2. **Motivation.** Motivation is the force that prompts individuals to pursue and sustain an effort toward a goal. Avoiding pain is a human tendency, but language learning requires a great deal of effort over a period of many years. Either activities that lead to language learning must be inherently pleasurable or the eventual goals must be so positive that they are worth the struggle. Motivation cannot be successfully sustained externally, with threats and rewards. Therefore, teachers should work with each learner to understand and optimize internal sources of motivation (Dörnyei & Ushioda, 2011).

3. **Facilitative emotional conditions.** Learning cannot succeed if students are anxious, worried, or feel threatened or overwhelmed. Under negative emotional conditions, the learner shuts down and is unable to take risks with language or attend to language forms. In contrast, a welcoming, safe, and relaxed environment is indispensable for language learning. Managing emotions in the classroom and supporting each learner to overcome his or her anxiety or negative emotional responses are essential teaching responsibilities (Williams, Mercer, & Ryan, 2015).

4. **Usable input and feedback.** Input can refer to how teachers present information. The term is also related to *comprehensible input*, which denotes language that is only one level above the language that the learner already knows (Krashen, 1985). Input beyond a learner's understanding can become usable when a teacher supports meaning through other means, such as visual aids, gestures, home language summaries, and the like. Another form of input that is key to acquisition is feedback. Without feedback, learners cannot be certain that the language they produce is understandable in its meaning, form, or pronunciation. A large body of research exists on the many useful varieties and relative efficacy of different types of feedback (Ellis, 2017; Ellis & Shintani, 2014; Lyster & Saito, 2010; Nassaji & Kartchava, 2017). Some types of feedback are clarification requests, explicit correction, reformulations, metalinguistic signals, and recasts. Prompting speakers to repair their own speech, also called elicitation of self-repair, is the most productive form of feedback.

5. **Deliberate practice.** Practice is the collective name of activities whose goal is to systematically develop second language skills (DeKeyser, 2007, 2010). These activities are not drills that demand imitation and repetition; rather, practice is a much broader range of activities that lead to fluency, accuracy, and automaticity of specific subskills.

Knowing language rules cognitively is not the same as applying them in real time, fluently, consistently, and without conscious awareness. Language proficiency involves moving focused attention on basic skills into accurately executed, automatic processes. Mastering a second language requires a complex skill set that takes thousands of hours of systematic, deliberate practice to develop (DeKeyser, 2007, 2010).

The foundation of effective instruction is monitoring and ensuring that all of the essential conditions of second language acquisition are met and sustained for every learner.

Beneficial Conditions

Beneficial conditions are those conditions that contribute to second language learning and work to the advantage of learners who have access to them. Some beneficial conditions depend on the context of language learning. Some can be enhanced by instructional practices.

1. **Relatedness of home and new language.** When we say that the first, or home, language is closer to the new language—in this case English—we mean that the home language and the new language have similar speech sounds and phonological features, have many cognates (words that have similar form and meaning), have the same basic word order, and use the same writing system. In such cases, learning the new language is significantly easier. Learning a new language that is quite different from the home language, such as learning Swahili when the home language is Bengali, is harder and typically takes longer.

2. **First language oracy and literacy skills.** Many first language skills are transferrable to the second language, including a large conceptual vocabulary (August & Shanahan, 2006). Although the names of concepts and related terms are different in the second language, understanding the concepts themselves can scaffold word learning in the new language. Other areas of language transfer include phonological awareness, understanding the meaningfulness of print, and use of cognitive and metacognitive skills. When students have these skills in their home language, learning the new language is easier.

3. **Avid reading.** Being a motivated, avid reader in the home language helps in acquiring a second language. Practiced readers decode words automatically. They are able to hold their focus on texts for long periods of time. These skills are preliminary for being able to allocate working memory to the task of word learning by not struggling with the decoding task. Avid readers also read more, which means that they encounter more words and meet each word more frequently, which can result in a larger vocabulary and deeper word knowledge. Skilled readers may have mastered transferrable reading comprehension strategies in the first language, such as inferring the meaning of new words from context or quickly identifying main ideas and supporting details (Grabe, 2009).

4. **Prior foreign language learning.** If a student has experience learning a foreign language or is bilingual, learning English will be easier for him or her. Bilingual students bring to the learning process prior experiences, self-efficacy, and strategies that helped them succeed previously (De Angelis, 2007; Ó Laoire & Singleton, 2009). They are able to draw on the language that they consider to be closer to the target language. They do not necessarily "understand" the differences between the language (or languages) that they speak and the new language, but they draw effectively on their intuition, and they are ready to "give it a go" (Rutgers & Evans, 2015).

5. **Cultural knowledge and the ability to read social situations.** Language and culture are intricately bound together; communication depends on gleaning meaning from contexts and assumptions and on being attuned to nonverbal cues. Being able to process situations, gestures, or unarticulated intentions correctly is important for inferring the real meaning

of messages (Lynch, 2011). Students who already understand the culture or have teachers who serve in the role of culture facilitator are at an advantage.

6. **Personality factors.** Research has identified a number of personality factors as facilitative for language learning, such as courage (shaking off fear, being willing to take risks), positivity (reacting with positive emotional responses to experiences), tolerance for ambiguity (experiencing partial understandings as "the glass half full"), and willingness to communicate in specific situations (Brown & Larson-Hall, 2012; Williams, Mercer, & Ryan, 2015).

7. **Regular access to competent speakers of the new language.** Although all types of interaction are useful for language learning, students gain more from interacting with teachers and proficient peers (Sato & Ballinger, 2016). Sometimes teachers assume that students have access to interaction with native speakers if they live in an English-speaking country; however, this is not always the case. Each student's circumstances are different, and making broad generalizations regarding individual students' actual access to competent speakers of the new language is not advisable.

8. **Having purposes and frequent opportunities to use the new language.** Having reasons and occasions to use the new language is closely related to the previous condition of having access to competent speakers of the language. But this condition matters even more than that one for language learning. It is also an achievable condition within most instructional contexts with careful lesson planning. Regardless of the educational context, lessons with collaborative learning tasks such as pair work, small-group work, and one-on-one coaching benefit most students.

9. **Integrative motivation in the speech community**. This is one type of motivation that deserves separate mention from motivation for language learning in general (Gardner, 1985). Students who identify with a speech community will work harder because of their desire to be a member of it (Pavlenko & Norton, 2007). This condition is powerfully supported by active measures to make English learners and their families feel included and integrated in the English-speaking learning community.

10. **High-quality instruction.** Effective instruction includes all the necessary conditions of second language acquisition, leverages beneficial conditions, and mitigates the challenging factors for language learning (NASEM, 2017). Chapter 3 offers a wealth of ideas for providing high-quality instruction that facilitates learning academic English.

Additional Factors

Most of the conditions that we have discussed so far are within a teacher's or learner's control and can enhance language learning. Several additional factors merit special consideration. These factors potentially hinder second language learning, so teachers should recognize them and try to minimize their impact with specialized instruction and suitable interventions.

1. **Older students.** The age at which a learner's exposure to the new language begins matters for the eventual outcome of language learning. Age effects have been the subject of much research since the 1960s. Ample evidence suggests that there are some limits on late-onset learners' development of native-like proficiency, particularly regarding pronunciation, but that type of proficiency is not the educational goal for most second language learners. Where age has the most influence is in secondary school settings because new learners of academic English have less time to acquire the language than younger learners, and older learners have much more to learn to reach the level of the academic language proficiency

of their peers. Nonetheless, dynamic bilingualism is achievable even for these learners (Birdsong, 2016; DeKeyser, 2013; Muñoz, 2011).

2. **Socioemotional factors and special needs.** The challenges that socioemotional factors and special needs present to second language learning can manifest themselves in many forms, including trauma, post-traumatic stress, anxiety, depression, speech and language disorders, and learning disabilities. Effective teachers actively screen and monitor for these, advocate for learners, and engage specialists promptly without relinquishing their own responsibilities to support every student's learning within their own classroom. For students with special education status, the law is clear that they need services for ESL and for their learning disability. The recommended approach is to use multi-tiered, evidence-based interventions that are culturally and linguistically responsive (Hoover, Baca, & Klinger, 2016; NASEM, 2017).

3. **Limited and interrupted formal education backgrounds.** One group of learners who face enormous disadvantages by definition are students with limited and interrupted formal education (SLIFE)—particularly if they lack literacy in their home language. It is imperative to identify these learners' educational needs separately from issues related to English language learning and advocate for intensive, accelerated, supplemental instruction that is designed to remediate delays in literacy and content learning (Custodio & O'Loughlin, 2017).

4. **Long-term English learners.** Many English learners fail to achieve the language proficiency needed to exit the English language development program even after many years of instruction in U.S. schools. Becoming a long-term English learner can be the result of many factors, such as incoherent or poor-quality instruction, low levels of home language literacy, transiency, or the challenges of adjustment to the new language and culture. Economically disadvantaged students tend to obtain this status disproportionately. Teachers should be aware of the potential long-term negative effects when ELs experience difficulties with initial adjustment, switch program types, or transfer from school to school (NASEM, 2017).

Review the list of essential and beneficial conditions as well as additional factors that may affect second language learning. Which do you consider when you are planning instruction? What could you do to give your students a greater advantage in language development?

When teachers pair their understanding of the conditions for second language learning with knowledge of each English learner's background, educational history, and personal characteristics, they can maximize the conditions that they control or shape. Chapter 3 explains in detail the process of designing instruction to optimize essential and beneficial conditions of second language acquisition and to limit the challenging factors to the extent possible within a specific teaching context.

Language Develops through Use and Interaction

Effective teachers understand that language development involves active learning. Students construct language; they learn to use language in the way that it is used when others communicate with them. Watching and overhearing speakers are not effective ways to learn language. Rather, through conversation, students establish joint attention with partners; they co-construct meaning, check their understanding, and ask for clarification. They can test their hypotheses about language forms and receive valuable, just-in-time feedback so they can make adjustments or learn something new (Mackey, Abbuhl, & Gass, 2012; Rex & Green, 2008; Swain & Suzuki, 2008).

Language competence is not an abstract skill or stored knowledge that may be useful some day in the future. Language competence is functionality—the tool for shared cognition, shared understanding, and cooperation. An individual's language competence is the accumulation of all previous language uses. The more frequent and varied learners' opportunities are for language use, the more functional, complex, and flexible their language ability becomes. This means that effective teachers prompt students to interact frequently, and they provide regular opportunities for students to use language throughout the school day in varied modalities (listening, speaking, reading, writing). They also encourage students to use and build on all their language resources, including relevant and strategic use of their home languages (Echevarría, Vogt, & Short, 2017; Ellis & Shintani, 2014; Johnson, 1995).

Specific examples of how teachers promote language use in the classroom include the following:

- Encouraging pair work and small-group activities
- Providing language frames and language models so that students can learn to articulate language functions (for example, they know what expressions to use if they want to agree or disagree, build on another student's idea, or provide support for an opinion)
- Giving students opportunities to take the time to formulate and practice responses before interacting
- Prompting students to annotate texts with their own explanations and responses
- Asking students to notice language forms in texts and to make use of them in their responses
- Assigning quick-writes to stimulate language use and to promote writing fluency
- Reminding students to discuss ideas and plans before they start a writing task

In short, effective teachers multiply opportunities for students' active engagement with the material through frequent language use, speaking, writing, and active reading (Baker et al., 2014; Dodge & Honigsfeld, 2014; Fairbairn & Jones-Vo, 2010; Gibbons, 2015; Short & Echevarría, 2016; Zwiers, 2014).

Literacy Expands Language Development

It is not possible for students in K–12 settings to achieve full competence in English without grade-level academic reading and writing skills. The vocabulary used in extemporaneous oral communication is a small subset of the English vocabulary. Grade-level vocabulary and the full mastery of language forms can be achieved only by engaging with formal written and recorded texts. To develop such English proficiency, learners must engage in extensive and intensive reading. Extensive reading, often with learners reading on their own, ensures that they encounter a wide range of vocabulary and language forms. Intensive reading is usually supported by the teacher and provides opportunities for building depth of knowledge of target words and linguistic forms, as well as the multiple encounters and multimodal practice needed for learning that lasts (Cloud, Genesee, & Hamayan, 2009; Fang & Schleppegrell, 2008; Gibbons, 2009; Grabe, 2009; Herrera, Perez, & Escamilla, 2014; Nation, 2008).

As teachers help develop the literacy skills of their English learners, they need to be aware of possible challenges that learners face in the process, such as an unfamiliar writing system, confusing and inconsistent spelling rules, a need for oral language connections, a lack of vocabulary knowledge, a low motivation to read, or a lack of background knowledge. These challenges merit individual attention:

- **Working with an unfamiliar writing system.** English learners vary in their knowledge of the English writing system, particularly if their native language uses an entirely different form of writing. Writing systems vary in the linguistic features of the language that they mark, such as vowel or consonant sounds, sound length, tone, or stress. Writing scripts vary from alphabetic (such as English, Russian, Greek, Korean) to consonants only (Arabic, Hebrew) to syllabic (Bengali, Gujarati, Thai) and to logographic (Mandarin). Harder than mastering the script itself is learning the specific language features that a writing system encodes. The English writing system, for example, demands attention to both consonant and vowel sounds but not to word stress, consonant length, or tone (Weingarten, 2013; Borgwaldt & Joyce, 2013).

- **Dealing with confusing spelling rules.** Because pronunciation often does not match spelling in English, students may struggle when learning to read. Consider the spelling variations for sounds that are the same (y<u>ou</u>, d<u>o</u>, thr<u>ew</u>, thr<u>ough</u>, sh<u>oe</u>, <u>ewe</u>, q<u>ueue</u>, fl<u>u</u>, tr<u>ue</u>). Although English has many dialects in which pronunciation is systematically different, the spelling of words remains the same regardless. Consequently, recognizing letters of the alphabet is a very small part of learning to read in English in contrast to the much larger part that it plays in those languages where the sound-letter correspondence is more predictable. To read in English, students need much practice in hearing and segmenting sounds (phonological awareness), mapping sound patterns to spelling patterns (phonics), and memorizing sight words. Teachers can provide better help to ELs when they familiarize themselves with the phonemes and syllable types in their students' home languages and become aware of the phonological features of English that are likely to be unfamiliar or troublesome to them.

- **Needing oral language supports to understand texts.** For proficient English speakers, oral language serves as a scaffold for reading. If children understand a story when listening to it, they will find it much easier to comprehend the story when reading it again on their own. However, if the text that they are reading is beyond their oral language abilities, reading comprehension becomes an extreme challenge, even when they can decode the words with apparent fluency. Therefore, it is essential that teachers talk with English learners about the content of texts before and after reading. In addition, by doing so, they will ensure that oral language and reading comprehension develop simultaneously (Saunders & O'Brien, 2006; Baker et al., 2014; Helman, 2016; Herrera, Perez, & Escamilla, 2014).

- **Facing too many unknown words in texts.** An important element in the readability of texts and second language literacy development overall is vocabulary coverage—that is, the number of different words in a text. Research indicates that comprehension of text read independently depends in large part on how many words a reader knows in the text (Nagy & Scott, 2000). For example, knowing 80 percent of words in a text might seem reasonable; yet, reading comprehension is virtually impossible at 80 percent of vocabulary coverage. For minimal reading comprehension, a reader should know 90 percent of the words, and for adequate comprehension, 95 percent. To be able to learn vocabulary or content information from a text, the typical reader needs to understand 95 percent of the words. For unassisted reading for pleasure—the most sustainable and rewarding reading activity—most readers should have 98 percent vocabulary coverage. These facts have important implications for teachers of English learners:

  —Reaching such a high percentage is very difficult for English learners working with grade-level texts, unless they are at an advanced level. Therefore, to learn *language* through reading, students need texts in which they know almost all the words, with very few exceptions. Their language development is best served when they read books with few unknown words per paragraph or a single unknown word in every third line.

To achieve this high level of vocabulary coverage, teachers need to make available for English learners modified texts that are suitable for their age and interest but are not overwhelming in the number of unknown words (Jeon & Day, 2016; Nakanishi, 2015; Nation & Webb, 2011; Schmitt, Jiang, & Grabe, 2011).

— When assessing the percentage of unknown words in a text, teachers need to recognize that English learners are often able to sound out words fluently without knowing the meanings of those words. For language learners, being able to decode—that is, sound out—text is distinctly different from comprehending it. Some teachers have students read aloud, but a better way to gauge their vocabulary coverage is to ask them to read shorter passages in the beginning section of the text—say, 100 words—and have them mark unfamiliar words. If more than 10 words are unfamiliar, alternative texts or additional supports are needed. Teaching students to preview texts to identify and gauge the ratio of unknown words when they select books for independent reading is also useful.

What to Do If There Are Too Many Unfamiliar Words in a Text

Ask a student to read a short passage of about 100 words at the beginning of a text and to mark any unfamiliar words. If the number exceeds 10, consider doing the following:

- Mark the key passages for the student to focus on rather than the whole text.
- Find alternative readers with controlled vocabulary.
- Supply bilingual editions, and mark strategically the sections to read in either language.
- Elaborate texts by inserting brief, comprehensible explanations of unknown words.
- Simplify texts by replacing some of the unknown words and sentence structures.
- Provide a bookmark that glosses the target vocabulary in the text.

- **Lacking the motivation to read.** Some English learners may not have had many home experiences with pleasure reading, so motivating them to read might be as straightforward as introducing them to engaging text. But some additional challenges to motivating English learners to read may exist. On the one hand, trying to read books that are far above one's vocabulary knowledge and oral language skills is frustrating. On the other hand, reading only "special" materials with limited vocabulary or with content intended for a much younger audience is boring. Instead, teachers should provide students with a diverse selection of high-quality reading materials that are appropriate for their age, including many bilingual books, and teach them strategies to select books according to their interests and vocabulary knowledge. Students should learn to become strategic about the choice of language, the fit of the books for their background knowledge, and their own purposes for reading. Sparking students' motivation to read and kindling their self-efficacy in reading widely are among the most important contributions that teachers can make to language development (Vardell, Hadaway, & Young, 2006; Hadaway & Young, 2010; Grabe, 2009; Herrera, Perez, & Escamilla, 2016; Turkan, Bicknell, & Croft, 2012).

- **Missing the necessary background knowledge.** Background knowledge refers to the information and conceptual understandings or schemas that readers bring to their comprehension of texts. Studies have shown that second language learners' content familiarity can compensate for linguistic knowledge at most proficiency levels. Conversely, lack of schema and relevant background will impede reading comprehension even for advanced language learners or for seemingly fluent readers. Readers can boost their reading comprehension by being allowed to select texts about topics that they care about because of prior experiences. When teachers know what each learner is knowledgeable and passionate about, they can match their students with texts that will enable students to use their background experiences to help with comprehension and with texts that will enable them to build their linguistic knowledge. This knowledge of their learners will also help teachers recognize when students are not able to manage texts on their own or without additional support before, during, and after reading (Grabe, 2009; Herrera, Perez, & Escamilla, 2014; Krekeler, 2006; Lesaux, Koda, Siegel, & Shanahan, 2006; Lin, 2002).

Obstructive Beliefs and Constructive Responses about Teaching and Learning English

No discussion of the conditions for second language learning would be complete without attention to an important, deep-rooted challenge: the beliefs that some educators hold about teaching English learners in U.S. schools. Without a doubt, teachers' beliefs influence the way in which they make consequential decisions about how they will approach the design and delivery of instruction. Unfortunately, a great number of misconceptions circulate about teaching English learners, and these notions do not match up with current research (Brown & Larson-Hall, 2012; Klinger et al., 2016). Moreover, research findings on second language acquisition are often not shared with teachers in ways that are constructive for teaching and learning.

Table 2.3 presents a summary of obstructive beliefs about teaching and learning English, paired with constructive responses to these beliefs, as supported by current research. By embracing the knowledge presented in the right column, teachers will plan instruction more effectively to develop students' academic language skills.

Sometimes these beliefs manifest themselves explicitly; other times they remain unstated, yet they guide teachers' decision-making and actions. Recognizing obstructive beliefs in our own actions is important. For example, we may be spending a great deal of time teaching students about sentence structure but not allowing them ample opportunity to use and practice these forms in the classroom. We may be limiting our language teaching to highlighting a few vocabulary items and expecting that students will memorize them on their own. We may be expecting students to pick up language mainly from teacher presentations. We may be oversimplifying our speech and the content we are teaching. Reflecting on our own teaching in light of these obstructive beliefs is a productive start. Helping to dispel them and promoting the constructive responses in our own classrooms and among our colleagues are worthwhile next steps.

The Role of Language in Identity

We must always remember to consider each learner as an individual. The way in which we use language is personal. Our identity is delicately wrapped in how we speak and interact with one another (Douglas Fir Group, 2016; Norton, 2013). Each of us is easily recognized by our voice, the characteristic intonation of our speech, our particular speech habits, and our accent. How individuals relate to our language use is important for our self-worth and bears powerfully on any potential relationship that we establish. The way in which we use language may serve to create common ground, or it can become a source of "othering." Othering is a mental judgment of an individual as "not one of us"; it positions a person as an outsider to the community, "a cultural other" (Sanderson, 2004). Othering can manifest itself in subtle ways. Even the interjection of the question "Where are you from?" into a conversation with an English learner may suggest to the learner that the conversational partner does not think that he or she belongs. These judgments are

Table 2.3	Obstructive beliefs and constructive responses about teaching and learning English
Obstructive beliefs	**Constructive responses**
The role of the English language teacher is to develop students' English language proficiency without attention to their bilingual abilities and bicultural identity.	Bilingualism enhances cognitive capacity, and bilingual self-identity is a strong source of motivation for second language learning. Effective teachers try to develop all of their students' competencies.
Students are either motivated to learn English or they are not, and students who are not motivated will not learn.	Motivation is a key element to successful language learning. Teachers can build a climate to support students' motivation and should explicitly consider how their instruction can enhance it.
Students should start learning English at a very young age. The younger the better for learning a new language.	Young and older learners bring different assets to the language-learning experience. Everyone should be encouraged to learn a language at any age. What is most important for learning are realistic expectations, abundant time, and many opportunities for practice.
Young students pick up language unconsciously and effortlessly. All they need is immersion in English.	Young students need a positive environment in which they have frequent opportunities to play with language, use it with conversation partners, and engage in meaningful, developmentally appropriate literacy activities that are scaffolded to support their success.
The fastest way to acquire high proficiency in English is through immersion.	Immersion may promote certain aspects of language—for example, pronunciation and the acquisition of social language. Immersion is not sufficient, however, for learning academic English—especially reading and writing.
Older adolescents and adults are rarely able to master a new language.	Older learners can acquire high levels of proficiency in a second or third language. Their pronunciation may not achieve native-like levels, but they are capable of comprehensible and accurate language production.
Students either have the aptitude for learning foreign languages or they do not. Learning English is not for everyone.	All individuals who acquired a first language can learn a new language. Even those who cannot hear can acquire additional languages. With the right method of practice, every student can be successful.
The role of the teacher is to simplify language input so that students can comprehend it.	When learners are at the early stage of acquisition, the teacher's use of simple and clear language can increase their comprehension. However, for learners to advance, they need to encounter and use language of growing complexity. Teachers should match the appropriate language to the proficiency of the student.
Students cannot comprehend grade-level content in English until they develop English language proficiency.	Students can and must acquire grade-level content while also learning the academic English in which the content is presented. To delay content instruction will hinder students from advancing through the grade levels.

(continued on the next page)

Table 2.3	Obstructive beliefs and constructive responses about teaching and learning English (continued)	
Obstructive beliefs	**Constructive responses**	
Students should use English all the time, even at home with their families.	For many families, using English in a family situation may be completely unnatural. If parents are not proficient in English, using the language they know best in interactions with their children is preferable. Home language skills and a large vocabulary developed through rich conversations and shared reading with family members can support greater success with the second language as well as balanced bilingualism.	
Students who learn vocabulary and sentence structure will be able to use English successfully.	Actually hearing and speaking a language are necessary to acquire listening and speaking skills.	
Students should focus on memorizing words and phrases.	Students should focus on using the language purposefully. Routine and patterned language are usual for beginners, but students need to construct and be creative with language to develop proficiency.	

consequential, potentially determining whether individuals feel invited to take part in all aspects of the life of a community (Pavlenko & Norton, 2007).

As teachers, one of our main responsibilities is to act mindfully to ensure that students feel accepted and included, regardless of accent or dialect or any perceived idiosyncrasy of language use. Effective teaching ensures that every student in the classroom community knows that their home language is valued and their multilingual ability is an advantage, even as it is developing (Cummins, 2001). Effective teachers are vigilant in their efforts to ensure that non-native-like-ness does not serve "othering," nor is developing language proficiency viewed or reflected as deficiency.

In fact, knowing two or more languages is a strength. Culturally responsive educators recognize that English learners are well poised to be fully proficient in more than one language, and the optimal long-term outcome for these students is dynamic bilingualism. Dynamic bilingualism is the ability to adapt to communicative situations and use more than one language flexibly and strategically to make meaning, depending on the audience, conversation partner, or topic (García, Ibarra Johnson, & Seltzer, 2017). One aspect of dynamic bilingualism is translanguaging, the strategy of switching between languages to accomplish tasks with others. Translanguaging can be a practical choice; it can serve to help others and convey solidarity or group identity.

Dynamic bilinguals are fully functional with communicative partners who use either or both of their languages. They can cross linguistic boundaries with ease, and they can participate in knowledge communities beyond these borders. Dynamic bilinguals are an invaluable asset in the community. They begin as emergent bilinguals—English learners who also maintain and continue to develop their home language. With support, they can experience their dual language skills as a functional resource and a recognized element of an ideal identity.

We know that self-image plays a powerful role in the motivation to learn a new language (Dörnyei & Ushioda, 2011; Muir & Dörnyei, 2013; Murray, Gao, & Lamb, 2011). To succeed as a language learner over the long run, a student needs to hold a clear, positive image of his or her future self as a competent multilingual person. This future image must be vivid and plausible, and, preferably, in harmony with the expectations of family and peers. TESOL International

Association supports multilingualism and multicultural literacy as an educational goal for all English learners, and promotes instructional approaches for the teaching of English that align with that goal. The three vignettes below show students who can use their home and new language flexibly and strategically, gaining not only content knowledge but also confidence in the classroom.

In the first vignette, Anita, a Hungarian-English bilingual, is sharing her homework with her second-grade class. Her task was to talk about a decision her family made together, add details, and illustrate the event with a drawing. Anita elects to use both languages to do so. (See a brief video on translanguaging at www.the6principles.org/K-12.)

Translanguaging in Grade 2

MS. CONNORS: *Tell us how your family decided on this trip.*

ANITA: *I wanted to go to the ocean. So I told my mom, "Anyu, menjünk a tengerpartra. Oda ahol a játszótér van. Ahol lehet hintázni." And my mom said, "Az egy nagyon jó hely, csak messze van." Then my dad said, "We can go to the ocean much closer." My brother said, "Oda ahol a nagy sziklák vannak." So we went there where all those rocks are and there is lots of sand also. You can dig with your fingers into holes and find razor clams. That's how my family decided on that trip.*

MS. CONNORS: *I really like how you told us this in the words that everybody in your family used. So you wanted to go to a far-away beach. Is that what you said?*

ANITA: *I really like a beach with a playground, but it's far away in Maine. We went to a beach that's closer. It doesn't have swings and slides, but you can go there in an afternoon.*

MS. CONNORS: *Show us your picture and tell us about the words you wrote.*

ANITA: *This is my family on the beach—my mom, dad, and my brother. I wrote anyu, apu, and Robi. Here is the ocean, the sun, and the sand. Tenger, nap, homok. And the razor clams that my dad got. They are called kagyló, but I just put clam. I am going to ask my mom how to write kagyló. Then, we are going to share the picture with my Magdi mama.*

MS. CONNORS: *Your Magdi mama must be very happy because you can write to her in Hungarian. Say those words again slowly, in your teacher voice. We can try our best to repeat them after you. Then, you can tell us how well we did.*

In the second vignette, Mateo, a dynamic bilingual sixth grader, is working on a word problem with Diego, who is an English learner.

Translanguaging in the Math Classroom

MATEO: *El primer ejemplo dice: A car uses 3 gallons of gas to go 96 miles. Express the miles to gallons as a ratio using different formats. Entonces, un auto usa 3 galones de gasolina en 96 millas. Vamos a escribir la relación entre galones y millas de diferentes formas.*

DIEGO: *Una forma es decir la razón 3 a 96 y otra forma es 3:96.*

MATEO: *The ratio 3 to 96, which we can also write as 3:96. Another way to say it is 96 miles per three gallons and 32 miles per gallon. 96 millas por 3 galones y 32 millas por galón.*

DIEGO: *Sí, otra forma es la fracción 3 sobre 96, y también en fracción común, 1/32.*

MATEO: *Okay, we can use the fraction 3 over 96 and the simplified fraction 1 over 32.*

In the third vignette, Ana, a bilingual fourth grader of Mexican heritage, volunteers to read to the class a book of her choice in Spanish. She reads the text in short segments and explains to her classmates in English what is happening in the story, highlighting for them some key Spanish words they may want to learn.

Dynamic Bilingual Book Sharing in Language Arts

[Ana reads aloud from the Spanish-language version of the storybook *Abuela* by Arthur Dorros, and then she explains what she has read in her own words.]

ANA [Reading aloud]: "Ella es la madre de mi mamá. En inglés 'abuela' se dice *grandma*. Ella habla español porque es la lengua que hablaba la gente del lugar donde nació antes de que ella viniera a este país. Mi abuela y yo siempre visitamos diferentes lugares."

ANA [To class]: *So the little girl is saying that she calls her grandmother* abuela, *which is Spanish for grandmother. Because her grandmother came from a country where they speak Spanish. She and her grandma,* abuela, *I mean, are always visiting different places. You can see in this picture how they get on the bus to go together to visit a new place. They are sitting together, happy and dressed up very nicely. ¡Me gustan sus vestidos de colores! ¡Van en un camión! They are riding a bus.*

Effective teachers are aware that learning languages is a process of self-exploration and self-discovery, and they understand that motivation to learn a language is bound up with the work of shaping identity (Cummins, 2001; Dörnyei, 2014; Norton, 2013; Pavlenko & Norton, 2007). Such teachers help learners kindle an ideal self that incorporates multilingual competence as integral to success. Their learners are not afraid to take on this challenge, and they possess the strategies to achieve this long-term goal. Effective teachers recognize that identity is dynamic; it can be shaped and formed by discourse communities, and, in turn, membership in these communities motivates learners to communicate in the valued ways of those groups. Integrating and including learners in the discourse community shapes their identity and motivation to realize their ideal self.

A Look Back and a Look Ahead

Chapter 2 presents foundational information about second language learning. The chapter highlights the following ideas:

- The English language has a prominent role in instruction in U.S. schools; however, English learners can learn content by multimodal means, and they bring their own preexisting resources for learning to the classroom as well.

- English language proficiency is legally defined under federal law as grade-level use of the English language necessary for academic success in the standards-based curriculum. The five TESOL standards for English language development include social, instructional, and cross-cultural communication, as well as the academic language of the core content areas (language arts, math, science, and social studies).

- The development of English language proficiency entails the control and length of utterances, the growth of vocabulary, and the mastery of language functions and registers. Academic English is an important variety of the English language, which requires grade-level mastery of listening, speaking, reading, and writing skills.

- English learners face some unique challenges with literacy development in addition to those that native English speakers face. Depending on their first language literacy, English learners may need to learn a new writing system. They may need to learn oral language and basic vocabulary at the same time that they are beginning to read. Keeping them motivated to read requires matching them with texts that hold their interest and do not contain too many unfamiliar words.

- Successful second language acquisition depends on five essential conditions: normal first language acquisition, motivation, facilitative emotional conditions, usable input, and deliberate practice. Effective instruction must guarantee these as well as incorporate beneficial conditions: frequent interaction, avid reading, skills transfer from home language literacy, and strategy instruction. High-quality instruction maximizes comprehensible input by building on the language that students already know, by giving quick feedback frequently, and by scaffolding their comprehension with multimodal input. Teachers promote motivation in the classroom by supporting student collaboration in a unified classroom community.

- Individual learners do not have the same challenges. It is easier to learn a new language if you have learned one before, if your first language is similar to English, and if you are literate in your first language.

- English learners need educators' backing to imagine and realize themselves as successful, high-functioning individuals whose abilities to communicate in multiple languages are valuable to the whole community.

Chapter 3 details the 6 Principles that undergird exemplary teaching of English learners:

1. Know your learners.
2. Create condition for language learning.
3. Design high-quality lessons for language development.
4. Adapt lesson delivery as needed.
5. Monitor and assess student language development.
6. Engage and collaborate within a community of practice.

As you read that chapter and explore the 6 Principles and related practices, apply the ideas about second language acquisition that Chapter 2 has presented. The 6 Principles derive from research-based understandings about how language develops in K–12 learners. Let those understandings about language acquisition serve as an essential backdrop as you read Chapter 3.

Also reflect on your own practice as you read about the 6 Principles. Consider what you know about your students and which aspects of their backgrounds may influence their second language development (Principle 1). Reflect on how you organize your classroom and bolster the positive conditions for language development (Principle 2). Evaluate how you keep students' language proficiency levels in mind when you are planning and delivering lessons. Think about the ways in which you convey content knowledge. Do you use a large repertoire of nonlinguistic resources and embed mini-lessons of key English language functions and forms that are especially useful for learning the content that you teach? Do you frequently incorporate tasks that require students to interact and use language in authentic ways? (Principle 3). Reflect on what happens while you are implementing your lesson, and how you make necessary adjustments through differentiation, scaffolding, or background building to improve student comprehension or task performance (Principle 4). Also consider how you go about continually monitoring your students' output of academic language, whether it be oral or written, on a class assignment or a summative assessment, to be sure that your students are making timely progress in their language development (Principle 5). Finally, reflect on how you continually develop and strengthen your teaching through collaboration within a community of practice (Principle 6).

Additional resources pertaining to this chapter are available at www.the6principles.org/K-12.

3 THE 6 PRINCIPLES FOR EXEMPLARY TEACHING OF ENGLISH LEARNERS

E nglish learners (ELs) in the United States represent a wide range of diversity. Students come to school with many different needs and abilities, and the number of ELs is rapidly rising in our schools. As a result, almost all K–12 teachers in U.S. schools have English learners or former ELs in their classes. Former English learners are still language learners—most critically, in the area of academic English—and they still need instructional support in the classroom. Teachers of English learners include ESL/ELD and bilingual teachers, grade-level classroom and subject area teachers, special education teachers, dual language teachers, bilingual teachers, and reading teachers, among others. Many teachers who have not studied for an ESL/ELD or bilingual teaching certificate or endorsement may need targeted guidance to work with students who are learning academic English at the same time that they are learning subject matter content in school.

As we read in Chapter 2, all students who have learned their home language can learn a new language, but doing so takes time, persistence, and deliberate, ongoing practice. Students need frequent opportunities for interaction so that they can test their emerging language skills and receive feedback on their oral and written utterances. As elaborated in Chapter 2, research has identified essential and beneficial conditions for language acquisition that teachers can influence in the classroom as well as challenges related to individual student factors that teachers need to be aware of.

Despite the challenges that teachers face in educating learners to a high level in both the English language and content learning, experienced teachers have achieved excellence by following key principles for effective English language education. This book presents these core tenets as the 6 Principles for Exemplary Teaching of English Learners. This chapter describes each principle and identifies classroom practices that are helpful in implementing and supporting it. The chapter also presents numerous examples that flesh out the practices and illustrate how teachers in K–12 classrooms may implement them.

The 6 Principles for Exemplary Teaching of English Learners and Recommended Classroom Practices

1. **Know your learners.**
   1a. Teachers gain information about their learners.
   1b. Teachers embrace and leverage the resources that learners bring to the classroom to enhance learning.

2. **Create conditions for language learning.**
   2a. Teachers promote an emotionally positive and organized classroom with attention to reducing student anxiety and developing trust.
   2b. Teachers demonstrate expectations of success for all learners.
   2c. Teachers plan instruction to enhance and support student motivation for language learning.

3. **Design high-quality lessons for language development.**
   3a. Teachers prepare lessons with clear outcomes and convey them to their students.
   3b. Teachers provide and enhance input through varied approaches, techniques, and modalities.
   3c. Teachers engage learners in the use and practice of authentic language.
   3d. Teachers design lessons so that students engage with relevant and meaningful content.
   3e. Teachers plan differentiated instruction according to their learners' English language proficiency levels, needs, and goals.
   3f. Teachers promote the use of learning strategies and critical thinking among students.
   3g. Teachers promote self-regulated learning among their students.

4. **Adapt lesson delivery as needed.**
   4a. Teachers check student comprehension frequently and adjust instruction according to learner responses.
   4b. Teachers adjust their talk, the task, or the materials according to learner responses.

5. **Monitor and assess student language development.**
   5a. Teachers monitor student errors.
   5b. Teachers provide ongoing effective feedback strategically.
   5c. Teachers design varied and valid assessments and supports to assess student learning.

6. **Engage and collaborate within a community of practice.**
   6a. Teachers are fully engaged in their profession.
   6b. Teachers collaborate with one another to co-plan and co-teach.

Principle 1. Know Your Learners

Kim Kanter is a kindergarten teacher in south Florida. She has been teaching for ten years and loves her job. One of her students, Juan Carlos, is having a difficult time adjusting to the classroom routines. Juan Carlos comes from a migrant family and is learning to speak English. To help manage his behavior, Kim asks Juan Carlos's father to meet with her. Kim proposes that she write home about the child's behavior daily. She suggests that on days when Juan Carlos has misbehaved, the father enforce a small consequence.

"What should I do?" the father asks.

"Oh, maybe you can keep him from watching television," says Kim.

"We don't own a television," the father replies.

"Well then, don't let him ride his bicycle," answers Kim.

"Juan Carlos doesn't have a bicycle, Miss Kanter."

"Well then, keep him indoors. Don't let him go outside to play."

"Miss Kanter, we don't have air conditioning. It's too hot to stay in the house all day."

Teachers can best adapt instruction to students that they know well. Learning about students is time well spent. Basic information includes the student's name, pronunciation and spelling of the name, native country, address, guardians' or parents' telephone numbers, emergency contacts, and health history. How will the student arrive and depart from school every day? Is the student an immigrant, a refugee, or a migrant? Or was the student born in the United States? What languages does the student speak, and how much schooling has the student had? If school records exist, teachers can ask for translation assistance to determine the accumulated amount of instruction that the student has experienced. This information will help in determining a learning plan and can clarify such misconceptions as Ms. Kanter had.

Learning about the students' cultures helps teachers form relationships with them more easily. Values, traditions, social and political relationships, shared history, geographic location, language, social class, and religion determine many aspects of personality and lay out pathways for dealing with the world (Nieto & Bode, 2011). Student classroom behavior will be determined in part by the influence of a student's heritage. Figure 3.1 indicates areas for teachers to explore when getting to know a new student and designing a learning plan for her or him.

FIGURE 3.1   Important characteristics to know about English learners

What teachers need to know about their learners' education, language background, and resources

Home country	Access to supportive resources
Home language	Learning preferences
Cultural background	Cultural knowledge
Level of proficiency in the four English domains (listening, speaking, reading, writing)	Life experiences
	Interests
Home language literacy level	Gifts and talents
Home language oral proficiency	Life goals
Educational background	Socioemotional background
Special needs	Sociopolitical context of home country

PRACTICE 1A Teachers gain information about their learners.

Teachers collect information about their students' linguistic and educational backgrounds to determine correct placement for students. They also seek to learn a new student's cultural and geographic background as a resource for classroom learning.

Examples of Practice 1a

Teachers conduct intake protocols. Many local school districts and state agencies have developed protocols to assist teachers in collecting the basic information outlined in figure 3.1. An article describing one intake process is located at www.colorincolorado.org /article/getting-know-your-ells-six-steps-success

Teachers collect and/or review linguistic and educational background information from the school's or district's home language survey (HLS). During the registration process, schools or districts need to administer an HLS, whose purpose is to identify potential English learners. The HLS is given to all incoming families on enrollment, not just those assumed to be bilingual. Three key questions often appear on this form:

1. What is the primary language used in the home, regardless of the language spoken by the student?

2. What is the language most often spoken by the student?

3. What is the language that the student first acquired?

Sample home language surveys in various languages can be found at https://www2.ed.gov /about/offices/list/oela/English-learner-toolkit/index.html.

A tool for districts to self-assess their home language survey process is available at https://ies.ed.gov/ncee/edlabs/projects/project.asp?projectID=4484.

Teachers conduct a needs assessment. Many states have a specific process in place for determining a student's ability to communicate, read, and write in English. Teachers typically use the local protocol or state language assessment for this purpose. Examples of state assessments to identify students who are English learners include the following:

- California: English Language Proficiency Assessment (ELPAC)
- Texas: Idea Proficiency Test (IPT); Language Assessment System—LAS Links, Woodcock-Munoz Language Survey
- New York: English Language Proficiency Identification Assessment (NYSITELL)
- Florida and other WIDA states: WIDA Screener or WIDA MODEL

Teachers organize and share information about learners. The collected information should be available to all of the student's teachers. Often districts have a shared database that all teachers can access. It is important to provide common guidelines for sharing information. If possible, gather the student's teachers together to communicate what you have learned to help determine an educational plan for the student.

PRACTICE 1B **Teachers embrace and leverage the resources that learners bring to the classroom to enhance learning.**

Teachers tap their learners' prior knowledge purposefully in their teaching. They try to determine what gifts and talents students bring to the classroom, what interests motivate them, what life experiences they have had that are curriculum-related, and what else in their backgrounds has influenced their personalities and beliefs.

Examples of Practice 1b

Teachers collect resources about students' home cultures and languages. Online resources will provide the most current information about your student's culture. Multiple sources are helpful. Bear in mind that culture is not monolithic, nor is it stagnant. Not all individuals from a common geographic area share a common culture.

Teachers engage with parents or guardians to gain knowledge about students' experiences. Home visits, translation services, and a warm smile are helpful in putting families at ease. Teacher questioning may be intimidating to families who are vulnerable in a new and strange country. Assure families that the information you seek about their children is for the purpose of providing the best education plan for them.

Teachers guide students in an autobiography project. As part of beginning-of-the-year community building, help all students gather and organize information about their lives—in words and pictures or through multimedia. Pair students to share their information with each other. Help students with limited English to talk about their lives with the class. Encourage them to use their native language as needed.

Teachers act as cultural mediators for students. When we provide opportunities for students to discuss differences or conflicts among cultures and analyze the variations between the mainstream culture and other cultural systems, we enable students to learn about and honor other cultures and clarify their ethnic identities. We help students develop positive cross-cultural relationships and teach them to avoid perpetuating prejudice, stereotyping, and racism. The goal is to create a learning environment in the classroom that encourages diverse learners to celebrate and affirm one another, work collaboratively for mutual success, and dispel powerlessness and oppression (Gay, 2010). (See resources for advocacy at ww.tesol .org/advance-the-field/advocacy-resources.)

Principle 2. Create Conditions for Language Learning

Loray James teaches third grade in a dual language classroom. This year her class has five students whose families have emigrated from Guatemala. The children are at varying language proficiency levels, but all of them are below grade level in reading and writing skills. Loray has decided to teach a social studies unit based on the agriculture, weather, vegetation, food, and customs of Guatemala. Her language learners contribute to the topic by sharing family pictures, recipes, and descriptions of the places their families lived in Guatemala. The children are very excited. Loray has never seen her language learners participate so enthusiastically in their learning. They love reading the books that she found about Guatemala.

English learners come from a variety of countries, speak many different languages, and may or may not be eager to leave the comfort of their native countries, their friends, and family members to live in the United States. Teachers respond to these very understandable anxieties by creating a classroom culture that will ensure that new students feel safe and welcome in the class.

PRACTICE 2A **Teachers promote an emotionally positive and organized classroom, with attention to reducing students' anxiety and developing trust.**

Teachers apply their knowledge of the positive conditions that promote language learning as they make decisions regarding the physical environment and the social integration of new students. They then begin to plan for instruction that will engage new learners and ensure their success.

Examples of Practice 2a

Teachers ensure that new students receive a warm welcome from classmates. Although new students may not yet understand English, they can interpret facial gestures. A smile is understood in all languages.

Teachers design appropriate work spaces. Many classrooms now have moveable furniture. To ensure that students will be able to interact easily with others, ask for help, and work together on assignments, classrooms can be arranged with tables or desks in pairs or groups of four to facilitate communication among learners. A section of the room can have computer workstations or space for students to do activities requiring movement, such as a task in which they physically form a timeline of key dates for an historical event.

When new students arrive, position their desks adjacent to those of other students and see that the new students have the materials necessary to participate in the class: notebook, pencil or pen, and other materials. Tour the school with new students to point out locations of lockers or cubbies, bathrooms, cafeteria, gym, art and music rooms, main office, nurse's office, counseling office, and other important areas.

Teachers organize the physical environment of the classroom to help students learn and use the new language. In elementary classrooms, wall spaces and bulletin boards are useful for displaying the alphabet, relevant vocabulary (with graphic support) and illustrations that communicate content information. In classes with beginners, classroom objects are labeled, in English and ideally in the native languages of the learners. The side of the board is a convenient place for listing the day's schedule, perhaps with icons to communicate the time for reading, science, music, and other subjects. In secondary classrooms, listing some common sentence starters and language frames or critical reading strategies on the wall can be helpful. At all school levels, teachers should set aside one place in the room for posting the language and content objectives, and they can present the day's lesson outline electronically or written on the board. A classroom library with independent reading material is valuable.

Teachers identify a mentor for each student. Peer mentoring helps new students learn classroom routines as they are guided throughout the day. The student mentor can help interpret the schedule for the new student, perhaps using pictures or gestures to communicate. Choose mentors carefully, with an eye to selecting learners with patience and compassion. The role should be celebrated and viewed positively in the classroom. Mentors need guidance as well as support from the teacher.

Teachers use clear, patterned, and routine language to communicate with new learners. Teachers' use of patterned speech and language learning routines can be very helpful, particularly with beginners. This practice is seen in action when a kindergarten teacher sings the same *It's clean-up time* song each day, a middle school teacher routinely introduces new vocabulary in only two or three ways, and a high school teacher provides oral and written directions with a demonstration when introducing a subject-area assignment.

Teachers invite and support students' home languages and cultures as essential to building rich understandings. Classroom displays, books, and other resources reflect connections between home and new cultures and languages. Teachers connect content learning with students' current and prior understandings—for instance, they identify home language cognates in a science lesson, have their students study the rain forest by looking at pictures from the students' native countries, or use culturally familiar goods to study of economic trading practices.

PRACTICE 2B Teachers demonstrate expectations of success for all learners.

Student achievement is affected by teacher expectations of success. A teacher with high expectations will exhibit positive behaviors toward students, motivating them to perform at a high level because of the personal relationship enjoyed between teacher and student. A teacher who has little expectation of student success does not communicate positive emotions or build personal connections that lead to higher achievement in school. English learners are subject to low expectations from many in the school community. Their peers realize that they are unable to communicate well in English and may be unaware of their proficient communicative skill in another language. To overcome potential biases, teachers must hold high expectations and communicate them clearly to all their students—English learners and other classmates.

Examples of Practice 2b

Teachers demonstrate the belief that all students in the classroom will learn language and academic content to a high level. They state these expectations clearly and consider in advance how they will scaffold learning to ensure that all students are engaged and successful. (See Practice 3b for a discussion of scaffolding.)

Teachers praise students for effort and persistence in order to communicate how success is achieved. Praise is most useful when teachers are specific in their comments. Saying "*Good job*" does not communicate exactly what the student did that was good. A better comment might be, "*I like your organization of the math problem on the page. Your computation is clear and complete. Tell me what helped you the most in completing this math problem.*" Praise of this sort will most likely lead the student to replicate the effort in math computation. Teacher language that values risk-taking and effort promotes a growth mindset (Dweck, 2006): *You got better because you practiced; You thought hard about that; Your effort is paying off; You figured it out!*

Teachers use a wide variety of instructional approaches to appeal to diverse learners. When teachers create conditions for learning, they consider student preferences and best practice based on second language acquisition research. This means that at times teachers may choose small-group or individualized learning. They may break down complex content and tasks into incremental, step-by-step processes. They may use alternative formats, such as computers, video, demonstrations, reenactments, and role-playing. They may augment learning with art or music or engage in cooperative learning projects. These choices are dependent on the needs and interests of the learners.

Teachers teach learners strategies to increase their abilities to participate in the instructional conversation. Interaction is critical for language development, yet some English learners need support to engage in academic discussions. Asking more advanced students to model an instructional conversation is one technique to use. Assigning buddy pairs or carefully forming small groups with strategically selected conversation leaders can facilitate discussion of content topics too. Teachers can also list key words and phrases that learners should use. Some teachers structure interactions by displaying question starters for partner conversations: *What do you mean by . . . ? Can you tell me more about . . . ? What does ___ mean?* (Levine, Lukens, Smallwood, 2013; Saunders & Goldenberg, 1999). Teachers should remember to ask students to process and discuss new content at every phase of the lesson, perhaps every ten minutes or so. By posing frequent questions on a new topic and requiring students to answer with a partner, teachers help learners to understand new concepts by listening to and explaining with another. Open-ended questions lead to more oral interaction.

PRACTICE 2C Teachers plan instruction to enhance and support students' motivation for language learning.

Language learning is difficult and takes a very long time. Children may not see the benefits of spending time and energy in learning English if the effort does not have an early payoff. Adolescents may not engage easily in language learning because they see English as outside their own cultural comfort zone or a threat to their identity. However, as the research discussed in Chapter 2 makes clear, we know that motivation is an important condition for language learning, so teachers need to expend effort to engage their learners and motivate them to work persistently at learning the new language.

Examples of Practice 2c

Teachers prompt students to make connections from their learning to their own lives. Connections with English learners' lives help them feel a part of the classroom experience and internalize their understanding of classroom concepts. For example, elementary teachers may ask students to interview family members to gather information for constructing a family tree. Older learners may relate their experiences with immigration when studying that topic from an historical perspective.

Teachers build a repertoire of learning tasks that students enjoy and experience as inherently motivating. Teachers continually add new teaching ideas to their knowledge base and select from them strategically to inspire students to learn. Some examples include game-like activities, tasks structured as play, experiential activities, storytelling, simulations, experiments, rehearsed performances, role-plays, songs, chants, and computer-based research. Online learning games can motivate learners in the practice of phonics, vocabulary, or math facts. When student choice plays a part in the selection of learning tasks, students are more involved and motivated to learn.

Teachers help students focus on a well-defined project with a future outcome to motivate and structure their behavior. Problem-based learning and project learning improve classroom dynamics by engaging learners in an important group project with a well-defined outcome. The positive emotions engendered by common ownership and the challenges of complex problems all help motivate learners for extended effort. Teachers choose projects and problems that have connections with students' lives—for instance, testing water samples in the school fountains, growing vegetables hydroponically in city environments, designing a new playground, or saving the town's remaining Gingko trees.

Teachers expect student ownership and support students in engagement with learning. When students are engaged in their learning, they process concepts more deeply. They are open to thinking out loud, venturing opinions, seeking comprehension, entering into discussions, and questioning to examine ideas. Teachers promote student ownership when, for example, they establish peer-to-peer discourse opportunities or when they ensure that student choice is considered in classroom learning opportunities.

Principle 3. Design High-Quality Lessons for Language Development

Mary DeCosta teaches world history in a bilingual high school in a large city in California. She has ten students in one of her classes who are in the process of learning English. In place of the written reports that Mary usually requires of her students, she has decided that this class will create video reports with accompanying posters. Mary writes out the unit objectives and explains them clearly and lets the students know that they can conduct the research by using English or Spanish sources. She also shows videos made by students from her U.S. history class that model the proficiency that she expects from her bilingual students. In addition, Mary meets one-on-one with her language learners and asks them to describe what they are expected to know or be able to do at the end of the project.

Lesson plan organization takes into account work in cognitive psychology. Knowledge, according to Mayer (1992) is thought to be constructed by the learner rather than memorized. Effective teachers design lessons that promote the development of learning and thinking strategies. Mayer lists three mental processes that are necessary to meaningful learning:

1. Selection of information to be learned and added to working memory
2. Organization of information into a coherent whole
3. Integration of organized information into the prior knowledge structures of the learner

Careful lesson planning can support the application of these mental processes when students are learning a new language and new content.

PRACTICE 3A Teachers prepare lessons with clear outcomes and convey them to their students.

Teachers can guide students to a lesson's essential language learning and content more efficiently if teachers and students are both aware of the important outcomes of the learning experience. Specificity and communication are key (Short & Echevarría, 2016). It is useful for all teachers to have language and content objectives in each lesson. Learning strategy objectives are also beneficial.

Examples of Practice 3a

Teachers determine language and content objectives for their lessons. Consider the following when planning:

- **To determine content objectives, ask these questions:**
  What specifically do I want my students to be able to know or do with the informational content by the end of the lesson? Is my objective grade-appropriate? Does my objective derive from a state content standard? Is my objective cognitively challenging? How can I communicate the objective to my students? Is my objective measurable? What contextual supports can I provide for learning?

- **To determine language objectives, ask these questions:**
  What specifically do I want my students to understand, say, read, or write by the end of the lesson? What specific language structures and vocabulary are necessary to convey the content? What grammatical forms do I want my students to use and understand? What language functions do my students need to use to accomplish success in this lesson? How can I communicate the objective to my students? Can my objective be measured? What contextual supports can I provide for learning?

- To determine learning strategy objectives, ask these questions:
  What learning strategy will I teach or demonstrate to help my students learn more effi-ciently? Is my objective measurable? Is my objective age-appropriate? How can I commu-nicate my objective to my students? (Levine & McCloskey, 2013)

Sample Language and Content Objectives

	Language objective	Content objective
Kindergarten social studies	Students will use adjectives to describe familiar objects with the sentence "*The [object] is [adjective].*"	Students will name and sort objects by use, for home or school.
Grade 4 science	Students will explain cause and effect orally, using "___*happened because . . .*" or "___ *is the result of . . .*"	Students will conduct an experiment to determine factors that affect plant growth.
Grade 7 language arts*	Students will propose an alternate ending for the story with a partner.	Students will identify the main plot and setting in a short story.
High school algebra	Students will explain orally how to graph a linear equation, using sequence terms.	Students will solve linear equations.

*Sometimes English language arts teachers ask how language objectives differ from language arts objectives because their curricular content is language. We suggest that teachers write language objectives to focus on the language forms and functions necessary to process or demonstrate knowledge of the content. Language functions are the purposes for which language is used (e.g., to describe, propose, compare, determine cause and effect). Language forms are the grammatical structures of words and sentences (e.g., irregular past tense verbs, comparatives and superlatives, complex sentences, adverbial clauses). Teachers can write language arts objectives to focus on reading and writing skills (Echevarría, Vogt, & Short, 2017; Levine & McCloskey, 2013).

Teachers communicate learning objectives to students. Simply telling students about the learning objectives may not be sufficient for many English learners. It is always preferable to write the objectives down, read them aloud, and then demonstrate what a successful outcome might look or sound like (Echevarría, Vogt, & Short, 2017). For example, given the language objective, "Orally explain the solution to a math problem using past tense and sequence words," a teacher might demonstrate how to describe the completion of a math problem in this way: *This is how I completed the math problem. I had to use subtraction because _____. First, I _____. Then I _____.* Content objectives can be successfully communicated in a similar manner. However, it may be helpful to show exemplars (e.g., sample essays, a poster exhibit, a well-documented science lab report) of the eventual outcome of a content objective or series of objectives in a unit.

PRACTICE 3B Teachers provide and enhance input through varied approaches, techniques, and modalities.

Comprehensible and enhanced input is necessary for communicating with language learners. To prepare to meet this need, teachers ask themselves questions regarding the implementation of the lesson, such as the following: *How will the new information be conveyed to my students? Will they listen to it, read it, or engage in research or an inquiry task to discover it? How can I support the input with context and scaffolding? How can I be sure that my students understand my input?*

Examples of Practice 3b

Teachers use comprehensible input to convey information to students. Comprehensible input is of primary importance for progress in the target language. Whether oral or written, comprehensible input helps English learners understand the meaning of the communication. Teachers scaffold the language input in multiple ways to aid learner perception and promote understanding. Comprehensibility scaffolds, explanatory devices for increased clarity, and modeling and demonstration techniques are among the many techniques that teachers use; these three types of scaffolds are highlighted in table 3.1. Multiple scaffolds can be used together to aid student success and increase comprehensibility.

Table 3.1 Scaffolding for comprehensibility		
Scaffolding for comprehensibility	Explanatory devices for comprehensibility	Modeling and demonstrations

• Gesturing and using facial expressions
• Illustrating and using visuals
• Simplifying (or elaborating)
• Relying on high-frequency vocabulary
• Embedding definitions and explanations
• Providing or asking for home language translation
• Emphasizing key words and writing them down for students to see
• Demonstrating or acting out
	• Visual aids, such as
	  ▪ maps, charts, graphs, and graphic organizers;
	  ▪ drawings, illustrations, and photos;
	  ▪ physical objects;
	  ▪ video clips
	• Audio supports and other multimedia
	• Highlighted or bold text
	• Bilingual glossaries
	• Picture dictionaries
	• Simplified English or home language summaries
		• Targeting and modeling the appropriate language register (academic language vs. social language; word choice)
		• Providing demonstrations of language in use (e.g., model student essays, sample completed projects)
		• Explicitly teaching about different genres and text structures
		• Conducting a think-aloud book or chapter walk

Typically, but not always, learners are first provided with comprehensible oral language input. If the learner has not yet acquired literacy in another language, oral comprehensible input is a required first step. If English learners are already literate in another language, teachers may decide to provide both oral and written input to them. The dual modalities complement each other and provide further support for meaning, especially for older learners.

School language uses an academic register. This is the register of academic texts and instruction. As we learned in Chapter 2, academic language is more complex and denser than social language. It has many abstract terms and offers limited support by means of graphics, pictures, or other forms of scaffolding. Consequently, English learners typically acquire social, or conversational, language first if they have sufficient amounts of understandable input. This is the language of the playground, the school lunch table, and hallway chats. English learners are able to avail themselves of the gestures, the high-frequency vocabulary, and the context of the social conversation to clue in on the meaning of the utterances. (See Chapter 2 for a thorough discussion of the components of academic register and the distinction between social and academic language.)

Bilingual and dual language classrooms provide multiple opportunities for English learners to receive comprehensible input. The native language is accessible, either through classroom peers or through teacher explanation. Content subjects taught in the native language may be retaught or reviewed in English. Having knowledge of the content enhances the learner's ability to make hypotheses about the meaning of the input.

Teachers adjust their language to enhance input to students. When teachers enhance input, they make it more usable for English learners, who may then perceive target features of the language more clearly. The enhancements used by teachers may be verbal or visual. For example, teachers

- speak clearly;
- speak at a slower rate for beginners and at a normal rate for advanced learners;
- use varied repetition;
- use gestures as clues to meanings;
- use word stress, intonation, and/or pauses purposefully (perhaps with exaggeration);
- recast learner language in ways that approach the target;
- contrast forms;
- avoid idioms, jargon, and slang;
- avoid rapid language and vowel reduction;
- write down key words as they speak;
- elicit oral production or elaboration from learners.

Teachers use multiple sources of input to students. When teachers add visuals or audio supports to written text, they increase the comprehensibility of the material. Peer reading offers further assistance to English learners who are struggling with text. Other sources of input include

- movies and video;
- internet sites and other technology;
- paired talk or paired reading;
- peer tutoring;
- small-group discussion;
- presentations accompanied by visuals, notecards, and peer support.

Teachers communicate clear instructions to carry out the learning task. Teachers use and teach consistent classroom management practices and routines throughout the school year in an effort to help students understand what is expected of them in a classroom and throughout a lesson. Teachers use simple directions with patterned language that they repeat each time. For example, teachers may gain the attention of students through patterned hand clapping or through simple attention-getting schemes (*One, two, three, eyes on me*). They use the same gestures with each direction (*Turn to page 33* while holding up the text). They use signals for behavioral management also: placing a hand behind an ear (to indicate *Listen*) or pointing to the eyes (to indicate *Look*).

Remember that multistep directions can be broken down into step-by-step procedures, with each step modeled as needed, depending on the language proficiency of the learners, and written, oral, and pictorial clues can further aid comprehension. If we want students to perform a task well, we have to begin by showing them *how* to do it.

PRACTICE 3C Teachers engage learners in the use and practice of authentic language.

We know that language use grows through interaction. In too many classrooms, students are silent, sitting quietly while the teacher talks. These classrooms are not effective learning environments for English learners (Harklau, 1994, 2000). It is by speaking, listening, reading, and writing in a new language that achievement gains are made. When classrooms are silent, students may not be actively engaged in learning. (See Chapter 2 for further discussion of how language develops through use and interaction.)

Examples of Practice 3c

Teachers elicit output from students. Listening, speaking, reading, and writing are interrelated processes that develop in a dynamic relationship. For example, listening to oral language input is a receptive process, as is reading. Both processes require an active and engaged mind to construct meaning from the speech or the text. Speaking and writing, however, are productive processes. Speaking helps English learners develop the ability to write in the target language.

Speaking a new language requires a high level of focus on grammar forms, vocabulary selection, and fluency in order to make the message understandable to the listener. Speaking helps learners notice a mismatch between what they *want* to say and what they *can* say. The learner adopts a "syntactic processing mode" as a result and modifies output to make meaning clear to the listener (Swain & Lapkin, 1995). To encourage learners to notice their obstacles in speaking—and increase their ability to speak—teachers find multiple ways to elicit output from their students.

Teachers create opportunities for learners to be active participants. Language is best thought of as a verb rather than a noun (Levine & McCloskey, 2013). As such, it is best learned while *doing* something with it—by being actively engaged with it as a listener, speaker, reader, or writer.

Unfortunately, not all school-based talk is productive academically. To support learners in achieving at a high level, teachers strive to help them make their talk accountable. Accountable talk requires that students exert effort to explain their thinking with evidence. It also requires that they listen and respond constructively to others while solving challenging problems (Michaels, O'Connor, Williams Hall, & Resnik, 2013).

Teachers can assist in productive classroom talk by using talk moves such as the following:

- *"Say more on that."*
- *"So, you are saying . . ."*
- *"Do you agree or disagree with that?"*
- *"Why do you think that?"*
- *"What have we discovered?"*
- *"What do you think?"*
- *"Who can add on?"*

Think back to the discussion of dynamic bilinguals and translanguaging in Chapter 2. Encouraging students to share their knowledge and ideas in their home language lets them use that language as a strategic resource. If they do not know the words yet in English but can convey meaning in their home language, they are not excluded from the academic conversation. They can demonstrate their learning while also being introduced to the English words or forms that they do not yet know, in the teachable moment.

In addition, teachers may establish collaborative grouping in their classrooms as another way of including all learners in the classroom conversation. Groups that are carefully constructed, with attention to gender, personality, language proficiency, and knowledge levels, can promote productive classroom talk. Some examples of tasks used in collaborative groups include peer talk, asking questions, shared writing, and dialogue journals. Elements that lead to successful group work (Gibbons, 2014) include

- providing clear expectations;
- establishing and modeling a clear outcome;
- providing grade appropriate content;
- integrating content and language learning;
- requiring talk;
- teaching group procedures;
- involving all learners.

Teachers use techniques to promote active language practice at every stage of the lesson. Many techniques assist teachers in providing variety to classroom lessons and encouraging productive classroom conversation (Herrell & Jordan, 2008; Levine, Lukens & Smallwood, 2013; Vogt & Echevarría, 2008). Different techniques are useful at various stages of a lesson, as illustrated in the examples in table 3.2.

Table 3.2	Language practice techniques throughout a lesson
	Language practice techniques throughout a lesson
Starting instruction	• Roving charts • K-W-L • Four Corners • Anticipation guides • Language Experience Approach
Building instruction	• Sort tasks • Sentence frames • Directed Reading-Thinking Activity • Reciprocal Teaching • Concept maps • T-charts
Application of instruction	• Dialogue Journals • Reader's Theatre • Text to Graphics and Back Again • Report frames
Concluding instruction	• Rubrics • Collaborative dialogues • Comprehension checks • Numbered Heads Together • Stir the Class

Examples, descriptors, and models of the strategies mentioned in Chapter 3 can be found in The GO TO Strategies: Scaffolding Options for Teachers of English Language Learners, K–12 (Levine, Lukens, & Smallwood, 2013), which is free and downloadable. www.cal.org /what-we-do/projects/project -excell/the-go-to-strategies

Teachers integrate language learning into content lessons and content into language lessons. Teaching-learning efficiency and the requirements of the language-content load require that teachers integrate language and content learning for school-age English learners. In doing so, they recognize that content learning has basic language requirements. Students are expected to be able to read about the content, construct meaning, understand and participate in classroom discussions, make inferences, cite examples of major constructs, and determine cause-and-effect relationships (August & Hakuta, 2002; Echevarría, Vogt, & Short, 2017). Content is also the vehicle for language development. So teachers with primary responsibility for language development incorporate vocabulary, reading, and writing activities that reflect the content areas that their learners study.

Each content area requires specific vocabulary and syntactic structures that may or may not overlap with generalized knowledge of English. Characteristics and challenges of the language used in different content areas are detailed below:

- **The language of history and social studies** has abstract, multiple-meaning vocabulary and complex sentence forms with embedded clauses, logical connectors, and reported speech. Passive voice is common, and subject referents are buried in the middle of sentences. Teaching methodology in the social sciences often relies on textbook readings that are dense and beyond the reading levels of many English learners. Teachers of the social studies use abundant scaffolding to help ELs read texts, and they employ oral language strategies to convey information. Dialogues, oral history, role-playing, RAFTs (writing scaffolds that clarify the student's role as writer, audience, format, and topic), and historical reenactments are some examples of alternative teaching techniques.

- **The language of mathematics** is specific, precise, clearly expressed, and logical. Mathematical language is a required aspect of standardized testing. English learners can succeed in math when their teachers employ extensive oral and written practice of mathematical reasoning in math lessons. Students learn how to initiate and respond to questions and discuss and explain math while using math vocabulary and grammar. The use of visuals, think-aloud modeling, manipulatives, frequent and varied repetition, demonstrations, and small-group work all promote mathematical reasoning and language.

- **The language of science** has specific vocabulary, and concepts require abstract reasoning. However, science has the benefit of being a hands-on learning opportunity. "Doing science," rather than reading about science, is an effective methodology for English learners. Through exploration of the world around them, learners are taught to make observations, ask questions, investigate solutions, and communicate results. The context of the "here and now" provided by laboratory sciences greatly promotes comprehension and achievement. Science teachers are effective instructors for our students when they model and demonstrate, use varied grouping, relate learning to prior experience, and use manipulatives, visuals, graphs, advance organizers, and active experimentation (Levine & McCloskey, 2013).

Teachers encourage language learning beyond the classroom. Although some learners may live in areas where English is not routinely spoken, teachers can encourage authentic language learning and practice through school-related assignments that encourage students to participate in activities outside the classroom. Possible options include school clubs, sport teams, Boys and Girls Clubs, and community or religious organizational activities. Useful input can result from attention to the media: film, TV, newspapers, and the internet. In addition, teachers can encourage language interaction through tasks such as interviewing, letter writing, and rehearsing scripted dialogues.

PRACTICE 3D Teachers design lessons so that learners engage with relevant and meaningful content.

Students are motivated to attend and participate in the classroom conversations and knowledge construction when teachers deliver lessons that engage them in various ways. Culturally responsive instruction connects content with the values, traditions, worldview, and shared beliefs of the cultures of the students (Gay, 2010). Teachers can use information about the social and cultural identities of students as a basis for school achievement. When these are recognized and integrated into the school experience, students recognize themselves within the classroom community. This is a powerful form of motivation for school-age learners.

Examples of Practice 3d

Teachers plan tasks that are culturally relevant and interesting to students. As we get to know our learners, we discover which ones enjoy working on group projects and which ones prefer to work at individualized tasks. But most students respond to variety and creativity in their learning activities. Students at different ages have different interests. Suiting the task to the age of the learner is always wise. For example, older elementary and adolescent learners are more adept and interested in using computers as part of their learning. Primary-grade learners are more likely to prefer to use art, music, or drama to share new concepts. Relating learning tasks to the native cultures of your learners ensures that they will become engaged in the classwork. For example, students from countries with a culture of oral storytelling will respond well when asked, *"Tell the story of _____—your country's greatest leader."* Students who value music and dance in their cultures can be asked to choose songs that represent characteristics of the fictional figures under study. When studying a natural resource such as water, students can research sources, uses, and threats to that resource in their home countries.

Teachers select materials that reflect students' specific interests. When teaching literature, many teachers choose stories from their students' literary traditions: myths, children's stories, folktales, novels, drama, film, national speeches, news articles, and other culturally relevant material. They may use texts in the students' home languages. In other content areas, teachers may be aware that their students respond positively to hands-on explorations in the sciences and role-playing events from history. They allow student choice in materials for research or independent reading.

PRACTICE 3E Teachers plan differentiated instruction according to their learners' English language proficiency levels, needs, and goals.

Differentiated instruction (DI) is an instructional model that provides multiple pathways to learning and offers differing challenges to a diverse student population. English learners' needs sometimes differ from those of the English-speaking population in K–12 classrooms. Teachers who differentiate instruction first learn the needs of their learners through observation and inter-action. Then they plan and deliver instruction based on those needs. DI requires that teachers scaffold instruction for student success rather than reduce the complexity of instructional goals (Tomlinson, 2014).

Examples of Practice 3e

Teachers build scaffolding into lessons for different purposes. Various forms of scaffolding help all students succeed. Teachers structure learning in incremental steps and provide assis-tance to the level that the learner needs to be successful. The assistance may be in the form of a knowledgeable peer, annotations in a text, outlines or other organizers for summarizing concepts, or bilingual dictionaries. For example, a group project exploring the Cassini space probe might be organized around multiple tasks requiring varied language skills. Some stu-dents could explore information on the internet, others could do text research, and yet others might create outlines of all collected information or assemble visuals from multiple sources. The material could then be organized for a TV show panel with each student in the group asking or answering questions about the artificial satellite launching. In this way, the content would be learned by all students, and they would contribute to the group effort at their varied skill levels.

Teachers employ grouping patterns designed to promote peer support, engagement, and comprehensibility. Buddy pairs and small groups are the most common forms of social assis-tance for English learners. Many teachers carefully choose the group makeup so that students have opportunities to participate fully and feel supported in their learning. Sometimes groups are arranged by home language or reading ability, or with a mix of language proficiency levels.

Teachers provide supplemental materials. Teachers may use texts at a lower reading profi-ciency level or home language texts on the same topic or content. They may rewrite the text to simplify grammatical structures or decrease density or provide summary translations. They may also introduce alternative activities for students not yet reading at the level of the text, such as oral reports, online searches, and oral interviews.

Teachers plan for appropriate challenge, depending on learner language proficiency levels. Teachers prepare to modify the language level of oral instruction if necessary and incorporate modeling and demonstrations in their lessons to support comprehension. They aim for cogni-tive rigor yet may develop a range of activities for student practice. By knowing their learn-ers' interests and levels, teachers can design lessons that challenge all learners to advance in their learning.

PRACTICE 3F Teachers promote the use of learning strategies and critical thinking among students.

English learners face the dual challenge of learning a new language and new content material at the same time. Critical thinking is an important element of content learning. As students learn, they are encouraged to think logically, analyze, and compare elements of the content. They ask questions and evaluate a statement, an argument, or a piece of writing. Learning strategies help students to attain this high level of critical thinking. Teachers instruct students in grade-appropriate strategies. They then give students multiple opportunities to practice using the strategies in different contexts. Learning strategies allow learners to control and direct their own learning. These strategies are conscious, observable behaviors or non-observable mental practices that help learners to be more efficient in their learning.

Examples of Practice 3f

Teachers teach a variety of learning strategies for specific purposes. Over time, teachers introduce learners to a range of learning strategies that they can apply as needed when they are trying to figure out meaning, complete an assignment, or review material. Different types of strategies have different uses and purposes:

- **Metacognitive strategies** enable a learner to plan for a task, monitor the work, and evaluate effectiveness when the task is complete. They allow the learner to self-regulate, and they have broad generic applications. Examples of these strategies include advance organization, organizational planning, selective attention, self-management, monitoring of comprehension, monitoring of production, and self-assessment (Chamot, 2009).

- **Cognitive strategies** involve critical thinking and are often related to specific types of tasks. For example, note-taking is helpful when listening to oral language input, and word grouping is useful for vocabulary learning. Other examples of these strategies include elaborating prior knowledge, summarizing, creating images, reasoning by deduction/induction, using auditory representation, and highlighting text (Chamot, 2009).

- **Social/affective strategies** are important for English learners because effective classroom learning involves cooperation with others and the ability to ask questions for clarification. These strategies also ease the anxiety that accompanies being a language learner in a dominant language group. Examples of these strategies include questioning for clarification, cooperation, and self-talk (Chamot, 2009).

- **Language learning strategies** help students learn the new language on their own. Examples are vocabulary strategies, rehearsal strategies, analyzing forms and patterns of English, paraphrasing, and substituting (Cohen & Macaro, 2008; Echevarría, Vogt, & Short, 2017).

Teachers design tasks for students to practice using critical thinking and learning strategies. Despite best intentions, more than half of teacher questions are at the literal or basic comprehension level. They require yes/no answers or responses of just a few words. As a result, they don't provoke higher-order thinking or elaborated speech. Teachers need to deliberately plan more challenging questions, problem-solving activities, and project tasks and regularly remind students to reach into their learning strategies toolbox to plan and guide their learning.

PRACTICE 3G **Teachers promote students' self-regulated learning.**

As successful learners proceed through the grade levels, they become increasingly autonomous and in control of their own learning goals and behaviors. They learn to self-regulate. Self-regulated learning involves three skills: forethought, performance, and self-assessment. Students set goals and employ strategic thinking with tasks, exercise self-control and self-observation during performance, and, finally, evaluate their performance and regulate their reactions. Self-regulated learners are in control of their learning outcomes (Zimmerman & Schunk, 2012).

Examples of Practice 3g

Teachers facilitate students' setting of meaningful goals for themselves and monitoring of their progress toward those goals. Many teachers accomplish student goal setting through individualized conferences with students that occur on a regular schedule. At these conferences, teachers can display evidence of student accomplishment to that point and then suggest various goals for future progress. Teachers may then enable students to make their own choices about how to achieve their goals.

Teachers provide self-assessment tools that allow students to evaluate their strengths and weaknesses. For young learners, a smiley/frowny face evaluation at the end of a learning task might be sufficient. For older learners, Likert-type assessments can help the learner evaluate performance in a variety of areas on a scale of 1 to 5. Rubrics are useful for learners at all ages. They help learners self-evaluate by providing a list of the specific criteria (tied to the lessons objectives) that will be used to judge a product or presentation. Various performance levels are modeled or described, using a scoring scale with numbers, letters, or other descriptive labels. When teachers clearly explain rubrics prior to the learning experience, learners have a clear understanding of what they are to know or be able to do at the end of the lesson. Learners can also work to self-evaluate their performances or products to achieve at a higher level.

Teachers help learners develop effective study habits. Effective study habits are necessary for English learners who are mastering content and language simultaneously. Many students do not know which habits are best, however. Teachers can identify effective study procedures at varying stages of language and learning proficiency and integrate these into the classroom lesson. Modeling and practice over a period of time will ensure that students have learned the procedures and are capable of using them. Productive study habits include

- structured note-taking;
- Word Squares;
- Question-Answer Relationship;
- Cornell Notes;
- concept maps.

Principle 4. Adapt Lesson Delivery as Needed

Jim Tudor teaches fifth grade in a suburban school in New York State. He has several students in his class who are currently learning English at various levels of proficiency. Jim uses cooperative learning as a classroom organization strategy as much as possible. He has noticed that his students are more involved in their learning when they have the support of another student to clarify, restate, correct, and model the academic language required of the grade level. This morning Jim is using a jigsaw technique that divides up the text to enable each student to read about one of the three branches of the United States government. Jim has provided questions for the students to answer about their section. Later, they will teach what they have learned to other students who read the two different sections.

The interactions between teachers and learners during classroom instruction provide teachers with a great deal of information about the effectiveness of their teaching. By observing and reflecting on learners' responses, teachers can readily see whether or to what degree the students are succeeding in meeting the learning objective. Often objectives are not met because of a variety of obstacles: the students' lack of prior knowledge, the teacher's incorrect assumptions about lesson delivery, staggering differences in the students' language proficiencies, pacing problems, and so on. If students are not succeeding, teachers need to reflect on the causes and make adjustments during their lessons. Similarly, if the lesson tasks are too easy, the teacher will want to increase the challenge. This decision-making may occur frequently on any given day, and decisions sometimes need to be made in a matter of seconds.

PRACTICE 4A Teachers check student comprehension frequently and adjust instruction according to learner responses.

To teach effectively, teachers need to evaluate what students know and what they do not know, in real time. We do not want to wait until the end of a lesson or the end of a unit to discover that our students have misunderstood a key concept or have incorrectly learned critical vocabulary.

Examples of Practice 4a

Teachers use teaching practices that ensure better auditory comprehension. Using a structure like 10-2 activities, teachers interrupt their oral input every ten minutes to provide two-minute opportunities for students to interact with the new learning. English learners learn best when they are not required to sustain extended periods of concentration while simultaneously attempting to comprehend auditory input. Lessons will be more effective if students are provided with opportunities to interact with others about the input. These two-minute breaks offer teachers excellent moments for checking learners' comprehension and can be used with all learners, throughout the lesson. Examples of 10-2 comprehension checks include Turn and Talk, Think Pair Share, Sketch and Share, and other targeted interactional structures.

Teachers check comprehension with group response techniques. Teachers can use quick comprehension checks during a lesson to gauge how the class is doing. Some group response activities include Thumbs Up/Thumbs Down, Response Boards (all students respond individually on a dry-erase board or sheet of paper and show the teacher), 3-2-1 for Self-Assessment, and technology options (websites and apps) using handheld devices or tablets.

PRACTICE 4B Teachers adjust their talk, the task, or the materials according to learner responses.

As a lesson unfolds, if teachers notice some confusion or misunderstanding, they make adjustments so that all learners can meet the learning goals. They may vary their oral language input to ease the comprehension load. They may help students gain access to other forms of input through the use of home language texts, translations, alternative texts, visual aids, and peer support. They might also adapt a task midstream, add more time, find supplemental resources, or pull a small group of students together for reteaching while the rest of the class works independently.

Examples of Practice 4b

Teachers modify their oral language input as necessary to advance comprehension and scaffold academic language learning. Examples of teacher adjustments include the following:

- **Simplification.** The teacher makes sentences shorter and grammatically less complex, eliminates idioms and slang, and uses fewer pronouns in extended talk.

- **Wait time.** The teacher waits to allow learners time to respond to a question. The amount of time depends on the type of question asked. Recall questions may require about three seconds, but higher-order thinking questions could merit a wait time of seven to ten seconds.

- **Open-ended questioning.** The teacher asks questions which require a full sentence utterance rather than a one-word response (Can you tell me more about that? What else did you learn?)

Teachers switch to other forms of input as needed. In addition to varying their teacher talk, teachers can offer other options for input, such as visuals, support of the home language from peers, manipulatives, movement, role-playing, and texts at different readability levels, to ease comprehension.

Teachers adapt the task to learner proficiency levels. The teacher may regroup students to provide support for English learners with their English-speaking or bilingual peers. Teachers might change a task to reduce the language load, as appropriate to the student. Additionally, they may adjust the product of the learning task so that students with developing skills are able to exhibit content learning in a variety of ways: projects, group tasks, tests, demonstrations, and so on. Assessments can also be varied to accommodate learners. Tools such as portfolios, rubrics, and oral language reporting provide a picture of the English learner's academic growth.

Teachers scaffold extensively to provide equitable access to content for all learners. Scaffolding has been defined as the *temporary* structures that teachers use to support learning. For English learners, scaffolds of various kinds are essential to help learners maintain goal orientation, reduce frustration, and move forward to developing new skills, concepts, and levels of understanding (Wood, Bruner, & Ross, 1976).

Grade-appropriate content objectives both support and challenge students when they are scaffolded to increase comprehensibility. Scaffolds come in many different forms and often change as student proficiency advances. They can be used in tandem to provide higher levels of support. For example, students who have been paired to read a text together can be given a graphic organizer to help them summarize the main concepts. In general, scaffolds fall into two main categories: material supports and social supports. A sampling of these supports appears in table 3.3.

Table 3.3	Scaffolding types: Material supports and social supports	
	Scaffolding types	
Material supports	• Graphic organizers • Diagrams • Pictures • Props • Sentence frames • Advance organizers • Outlines • Structured notes	• Two-column charts (e.g., main ideas on left, supporting details on right) • Picture dictionaries • Learner dictionaries • Translation dictionaries • Word source software • Alternative and modified texts • Home language texts
Social supports	• Small-group learning • Interactively structured conversations (e.g., buddy talk, Think Pair Share) • Cooperative learning structures (e.g., Numbered Heads Together, jigsaw)	• Group work with designated roles (e.g., reciprocal teaching, roundtable, round robin) • Study buddies • Study groups • Home language partners

At times, learning strategies can provide scaffolding for students who use them to help organize their learning, focus on aspects of language, determine the meaning of unfamiliar words, and memorize. Table 3.4 provides a sampling of such learning strategies.

Table 3.4	Learning strategy scaffolds	
	Learning strategies that scaffold learning	
Metacognitive and cognitive strategies	• Note taking • Selective listening and reading • Summarizing • Organizational planning	• Effective memorization • Prediction • Advance organization • Annotating
Vocabulary strategies	• Making personal dictionaries • Grouping and categorizing words • Visualization • Analysis of word parts • Deducing meaning from context and part of speech	• Self-assessment • Substituting a known word for an unknown one

Principle 5. Monitor and Assess Student Language Development

Sally Hong is delighted to have a new Korean student in her first-grade classroom. The little girl loves to talk. Unfortunately, her English is quite limited, and Sally never learned the Korean language from her grandparents.

Penny: I gob new bab sut.

Sally Hong: Oh, do you have something new? What is it?

Penny: New bab sut.

Sally Hong: Is it a new baby?

Penny: No, bab sut.

Sally Hong: What do you do with this new thing?

Penny: Swim.

Sally Hong: Oh, you have a new bathing suit. You're going to swim in your new bathing suit. Tell me what it looks like.

English learners advance to differing levels of language proficiency in varied ways. Certain learners are comfortable with speaking English haltingly and ungrammatically at an early stage of learning. Other students wait until they are sure of being understood and certain of their grammatical competency. To advance their students' learning efficiently, teachers need to be aware of their capacities for comprehending and speaking English. Constant monitoring and assessment, built into daily instruction, will provide the best evidence for language growth.

PRACTICE 5A Teachers monitor student errors.

By interacting frequently with our students, we can acquire a great deal of information about their progress. Some teachers record the results of their interactions (e.g., correct and incorrect uses of English) in an anecdotal way, use a check list, or simply change student grouping patterns and/or partners, depending on their newly developing proficiency.

Examples for Practice 5a

Teachers take note of errors to provide appropriate feedback to students. Sometimes learners' errors are simply mistakes caused by lack of attention or lack of competence. Other errors are developmental. These errors indicate that the learner has incomplete learning about the features of the target language. Some errors involve negative transfer from the native language, such as incorrect word order. Teachers are aware of error causation and provide appropriate remediation and/or feedback. They do not have to directly address developmental errors related to language features not yet learned, but they can model correct speech or written text.

Teachers reteach when errors indicate that students misunderstood or learned the material incorrectly. When errors are not part of the language development process, teachers plan for reteaching or additional practice. They may present a mini-lesson on the topic for the whole class or work with a small group of learners who need the support.

PRACTICE 5B Teachers provide ongoing effective feedback strategically.

Effective feedback has defined characteristics. To be constructive, a teacher's oral feedback in response to a learner's error is best modulated in delivery and tone, depending on the age of the learner and the classroom situation. Teachers determine feedback on the basis of their observation of student behavior. The feedback can be positive or corrective. It is important that the feedback be specific and related to what learners are doing well in addition to what they can improve (see examples of positive feedback in the Examples for Practice 2b).

Examples for Practice 5b

Teachers use specific feedback. Specific feedback that highlights the error in some way leads to better performance than general feedback. Teacher modeling is one form of specific feedback. Products and presentations can be modeled prior to learning and used for comparison afterward. Demonstrations are also helpful in showing how to perform at a high level. For project work, rubrics are very effective in identifying specifically how students can achieve success, as long as the rating criteria have been explained to students in advance.

Teachers deliver feedback in a timely manner. Students may be more able to use feedback if it is not delayed. Timeliness is more important with oral feedback than with written feedback. Private feedback is appreciated by all students, no matter their age. For older learners, a feedback focus is helpful for teacher and learner. Some teachers determine the feedback focus in consultation with the student. The focus is defined, and a time period is determined for observation (as for speech in a particular setting) or review (as for written work).

Teachers deliver feedback according to the age and proficiency level of the learner. Young children are less capable of responding to large amounts of feedback, especially if they consider the feedback to be negative. They are, however, open to positive feedback—the type that specifically points out what they are doing correctly and encourages them to continue the beneficial behavior. Separating positive and negative feedback helps learners of all ages concentrate more clearly on teacher message. Similarly, feedback must match the proficiency level of the student. For example, if a beginner has just learned the simple present tense, feedback suggesting that he or she use an irregular past tense verb form is inappropriate.

Teachers use a variety of types of oral corrective feedback. Corrective feedback allows learners an opportunity to notice the differences between their language and the language of the teacher. Oral feedback occurring in teacher-student interactions is generally of three main types: explicit corrections, recasts, and prompts for self-repair. Research indicates that output-oriented feedback (where the student produces the correction) is more effective than input-oriented feedback (where the teacher provides the correction). Prompts are especially beneficial in content-based classrooms. They work well when students receive feedback on grammatical errors (that have been taught and are developmentally appropriate). Prompts push students to self-repair and have been shown to lead to more accurate output (Lyster & Saito, 2010). The three types of oral feedback are illustrated below:

1. **Explicit corrections** occur when the teacher indicates to students that they have made an error and supplies a correction.

   — Student: *The wood . . . the wood go down in the water.*

   — Teacher: *Do you mean the wood went down? We say the wood **sank** in the water.*

2. **Recasts** occur after students' utterances. The teacher reformulates all or part of the utterance.

   — Student: *The wood no float.*

   — Teacher: *The wood doesn't float.*

3. **Prompts for self-repair** signal students to attempt to repair an utterance on their own. Such prompts can be of many types: repetitions, direct elicitations, clarification requests, metalinguistic clues, open-ended questions, and non-verbal cues (Lyster & Saito, 2010).

— **Repetition.** The teacher repeats the learner's utterance, often with exaggeration or inflection to indicate a problem. (Student: *The wood go down.* Teacher: *The wood go down?*)

— **Elicitation.** The teacher elicits the correct form by asking specific questions, pausing, or asking for a reformulation. (*How do we say that in English?*)

— **Clarification request.** The teacher uses a phrase to indicate that the learner's utterance was not understood. (*Excuse me? I don't understand. Can you tell me again?*)

— **Metalinguistic clues.** The teacher asks questions to indicate that the form of the utterance is not correct (e.g., verb form, plurality). (*You need to use the past tense.*)

— **Open-ended questions.** The teacher asks general questions that allow the learner to select the information that he or she will talk about. (*Tell me what you know about . . . ? What did you discover about . . . ? What can you tell me about . . . ?*)

— **Non-verbal cues.** The teacher's quizzical facial expressions and/or gestures may serve as prompts for self-repair.

Teachers use written feedback when appropriate. Teachers share their insights, opinions, recommendations, and suggestions, with the goal of helping students improve their writing skills. Corrective feedback can take many different forms to help students reflect on their learning more deeply and develop self-regulation processes. In the task of writing, teachers often use a collaborative approach to the revision process. By collaborating with students, teachers can help them reflect on their strengths and weaknesses in each draft and ask for specific help in making improvements. Various ways of achieving this goal include the use of teacher-student memos, portfolios, and learning journals (Andrade & Evans, 2013). Older learners can be taught procedures for peer editing as well.

PRACTICE 5C Teachers design varied and valid assessments and supports to assess student learning.

The K–12 educational community in the United States is awash in testing. Many teachers complain that the amount of testing is eroding instructional time. In addition, some teachers feel that required testing doesn't accurately reveal what students have learned in their classrooms. This is especially true of beginning and intermediate English learners who have not yet reached the level of proficiency necessary for standardized testing. Teachers of English learners prefer that their students be assessed through classroom-based assessment instruments that mirror instruction and are discrete enough to show the progress being made.

Examples of Practice 5c

Teachers use classroom-based assessment to inform teaching and improve learning. The purpose of classroom-based assessment is to gather information regarding learning over a period of time. Teachers are careful to assess language growth apart from content learning. Classroom-based assessment can inform our teaching by helping us become better acquainted with our students' growth in specific skill areas. As a result, it can lead to improvement in our students' learning experience.

Examples of classroom-based assessments include teacher observations, teacher developed tests, comprehension checks, and rubrics for student products (such as writing projects, presentations, and multimedia products), checklists, surveys/questionnaires, and anecdotal records. Classroom-based assessment is integrated into instruction. It often provides students with feedback about their progress both in language and content and can be used to communicate more effectively with parents and other school personnel (Levine & McCloskey, 2013).

Teachers use testing procedures based on principles of assessment. Basic evaluation principles are that assessments should be fair, reliable, and valid.

- **Fairness** requires that all students have an equal chance to show what they know and can do. Fairness does not require that all students be treated in the same way. In fact, for English learners, it would be unfair to assess them in the same way as English speakers. That type of assessment often leads to frustration and failure. To achieve some degree of fairness in classroom-based testing, teachers provide scaffolds. They may scaffold a math assessment, for example, by providing models of problem solving. They allow students to work in buddy pairs to negotiate the meaning of the questions. They provide oral language practice in describing word problems before moving on to the writing phase of the lesson. Consider the following questions to determine whether your classroom assessments are fair:
    - Did the student sufficiently understand the questions asked?
    - Am I evaluating the student's content understanding or language development?
    - Does my assessment reflect my instructional practices?
    - Did I provide appropriate scaffolding?
    - Have I told students what I am evaluating and modeled a desired product?
    - Have I clearly specified the criteria on which the evaluation is based?
    - Am I evaluating the process, the product, or both?

- **Reliability** indicates that the results of an assessment are consistent over a period of time when scored by different raters. Holistic or analytic scoring of writing samples is reliable when raters are trained in the same techniques and achieve similar scores. Oral language scoring can be more reliable when raters use an observational matrix that is specific enough to provide dependable results.

- **Validity** is achieved when instruments measure what they are intended to measure. It is difficult to achieve valid results with English learners on standardized tests, particularly those written in English. Testing products may exhibit cultural or experiential bias toward students with different life experiences. Moreover, the test results are often influenced by the learner's limited academic language knowledge. Because of this, it is good practice for teachers to collect multiple sources of information about a student. Classroom-based, informal assessment that is varied and reflects the classroom teaching style can best achieve a broad and valid picture of the learner's skills and knowledge (Levine & McCloskey, 2013).

Teachers rely on a variety of assessment types to determine student achievement. Although informal assessments are typically fairer and more valid, formal assessments are required by district and state educational authorities. Standardized testing will frequently present a skewed picture of an English learner's achievement, particularly at lower levels of proficiency. The picture would be more complete if multiple informal assessments are included in the assessment package. Furthermore, if a student is allowed accommodations on the formal test, the teacher needs to use the same accommodations in the classroom. These types of assessment include the following:

- **Formative assessment** occurs as teachers gather information about student learning during the instructional process. Formative assessment is ongoing, occurs during instruction, and guides the teaching process. Much formative assessment is informal and occurs on the spot (Echevarría, Vogt, & Short, 2004). Other formative assessments are conducted to evaluate teaching and learning objectives. They may be graded, marked on a checklist, written as anecdotal notes, recorded as oral speech, or collected through short quizzes, essays, and presentations.

- **Summative assessment**, in contrast to formative assessment, is usually conducted at the end of a long period of learning (a semester or year) and is more formal in tone. Standardized testing and district testing are examples of summative assessment. Although English learners are required to take part in summative assessment, states and districts often permit some learners to have accommodations. Accommodations represent changes in the testing situation or in the test itself that increases a student's access to the content of the test while preserving test validity (Rivera, 2006). Accommodations may include (but not be limited to)

  — extended time for testing;

  — use of a glossary or dictionary (English, bilingual, or customized) except with English language arts or English language proficiency tests;

  — a separate setting with an ESL/ELD teacher as proctor;

  — translated or extended explanations of the test directions;

  — test directions and/or questions read aloud (Levine & McCloskey, 2013).

- **Performance-based portfolios** give teachers access to multiple writing pieces collected over a period of time. A portfolio may contain different genres of writing and reflect editing and rewriting processes. Consequently, a portfolio can provide an excellent picture of the growth of a student's language skill over time.

- **Criterion-based rubrics** are useful tools for assessment and learning. They list the specific criteria used to evaluate a performance or a product and then indicate performance levels on a scoring scale that uses numbers, letters, or other descriptive labels. Rubrics are presented by the teacher prior to the learning experience and provide the learner with clear explanations and examples so that all learners will understand the criteria. Often rubrics are accompanied by models of excellent, acceptable, and unacceptable products (Levine & McCloskey, 2013).

Principle 6. Engage and Collaborate within a Community of Practice

Laura and Marina both teach in a middle school pull-out program for English learners. They share a very large classroom. When the bell rings for their planning period, Laura and Marina get together and reflect on their latest teaching experiments. They describe to each other the strategies that they have just tried and the results. Their conversations invigorate their teaching, and they are constantly learning tips from each other that they are eager to try in their own classes. After only three years in the classroom, both teachers have acquired a large set of techniques and have embarked on the road to critical reflection on their teaching.

A community of practice comprises people who share a profession and engage with one another in collectively learning more about that profession. These communities are becoming more widespread throughout K–12 education. No one can know all there is to know about educating diverse learners and, collectively, all of us are smarter than one of us alone (Lave & Wenger, 1991). We often begin our journey to professionalism by looking outside of our own skill set and exploring the knowledge base of other teachers in our schools. In this way, we can add to our repertoire of teaching techniques. For example, the special education teacher can show us ways to help learners focus on and recognize sight words. The bilingual teacher can help us understand the structures of our students' home languages and the cultures from which our students come. The reading teacher has wide knowledge of readability levels and text types. The science and math teachers know the critical vocabulary necessary for understanding their content. By sharing with one another, we expand and grow together.

PRACTICE 6A Teachers are fully engaged in their profession.

Although all teachers would like to believe that they were fully prepared for the challenges of the profession on the first day of their teaching careers, few of us really believe that. The more time that teachers spend engaging with the act of teaching, the more they feel the need to develop and grow to provide the best instruction for their students. What does it mean to be fully engaged in the profession of second language education? (See Chapter 4 for additional discussion on this topic.)

Examples of Practice 6a

Teachers engage in reflective practice to grow professionally. Dewey (1933) discussed reflective practice in his exploration of experience, interaction, and reflection; and later Schon (1990) enlarged on the notion by defining reflective practice as the process through which professionals learn from their experiences and gain insights into themselves and their practice. Schon differentiated between reflection *in* action and reflection *on* action. Reflection in action occurs when teachers reflect on a teaching or learning behavior as it occurs. Reflection on action involves reflecting after the event: reviewing, analyzing, and evaluating the situation.

Reflection in action calls for self-observation as we teach, monitoring the choices we make and then recording notes on completion of the lesson. This is the skill of critical inquiry. Some teachers use a journal for daily reflections. Others write anecdotally with the idea of sharing the experience with a peer.

Reflection on action requires that teachers have solitary time to think about the lesson and to reflect on what occurred, why it happened, how the teaching behavior related to theory or background knowledge, and what ideas it might suggest for future teaching situations. This is the skill of self-reflection. During this time, we examine our assumptions of everyday practice and evaluate them. The process can be distilled into three essential questions:

- *What did I do?*
- *How did it go?*
- *What did I learn?*

Reflective practice, sometimes called critical reflection, can lead to positive professional growth: "Unless teachers develop the practice of critical reflection, they stay trapped in unexamined judgments, interpretations, assumptions, and expectations. Approaching teaching as a reflective practitioner involves fusing personal beliefs and values into a professional identity" (Larrivee, 2000, p. 293). Teachers who engage in cyclical critical reflection become teachers who constantly test hypotheses about teaching and learning and experiment with these hypotheses in light of the context of the learning and the students who are affected. In this way, these teachers are constantly renewed and steadily increase their professional competency.

Teachers participate in continuous learning and ongoing professional development. The challenges of teaching and the diversity of our students increase every day. Our response to these challenges is to be continually working toward professional involvement and lifelong learning. Initially, individual interest will guide our engagement in learning—a love of music, a need for increased literacy training, an interest in other cultural groups, or a critical shortage of behavior management techniques.

Through personal learning networks, developed among other ESL/ELD, bilingual, dual language, and content-area teachers in our schools, we can question, share experiences, design workshops, develop study groups, pursue online training, write curriculum units, and talk about our classroom experiences: *What I did today, and what I learned as a result.* These conversations are too rare in time-pressed school days. But they lead to the reflection and development that are so necessary in our teaching lives.

Through participation in professional development associations, we can stay abreast of best practices. We can join a professional English teaching organization like TESOL or the National Association of Bilingual Education (NABE) or a content-specific organization like the National Council of Teachers of Mathematics (NCTM), the National Science Teachers Association (NSTA), or the National Council for the Social Studies (NCSS), and then get involved with one of the organization's committees. We can attend and/or present at local, state, or national conferences or sponsored academies and symposia. We can also read and write for the publications of these organizations to get new insights and exchange ideas.

In addition, we can pursue learning options in specific skill areas related to teaching—technology, curriculum development, or assessment, for example. We can do online courses and webinars, or apply for a grant, fellowship, or award to do language research or pursue a graduate degree. The list is long but lifelong learning takes time. We need to invest our personal time, and often our money, to become dynamic and effective teachers of English learners.

PRACTICE 6B **Teachers collaborate with one another to co-plan and co-teach.**

Increasingly school districts are moving toward an inclusion-based model of instruction in which collaboration and co-teaching play a large role (Staehr Fenner, 2016). Language and content learning are increasingly interconnected in K–12 classrooms across the United States. As a result, collaboration and co-teaching among ESL/ELD teachers, special education teachers, bilingual and dual language teachers, reading teachers, and content area teachers is essential (Valdés, Kibler, & Walqui, 2014).

Examples of Practice 6b

Teachers meet with colleagues regularly to co-plan for future learning. Time is the most valuable commodity during the school day. Teachers' schedules rarely permit them to have lengthy meetings within their own grade levels or teams. It is challenging for ESL/ELD teachers to find opportunities for mutual planning on a grade level, within a team of content teachers, or with selected content teachers in a secondary setting. In spite of the challenge, ESL/ELD teachers need to become co-planners to ensure their students' success in developing English language and content proficiency. These planning opportunities permit ESL/ELD teachers to become aware of the extent of the content learning required for students. They also allow ESL/ELD teachers to share information about students' language proficiency with content teachers. Some schools are able to schedule shared planning time for ESL/ELD and content teachers. When that is not possible, teachers often share information during break time, lunch time, or before or after school. The school administrators can help by making certain that scheduling allows teachers to co llaborate with colleagues for planning.

Teachers develop and strengthen relationships with school colleagues that facilitate co-teaching. Teaching in the classroom of another teacher can be anxiety producing. Co-teaching requires a level of trust on the part of both teachers. Co-teachers need to assure each other that they appreciate the collegiality and support that co-teaching can offer. The personal relationships that ESL/ELD teachers develop with colleagues are imperative to a collegial partnership. Co-teachers are not in the classroom to "fix each other" but rather to share skills and knowledge that will help all learners achieve at a high level (Dove & Honigsfeld, 2017). Co-teaching is a skill that develops over time and requires a level of expertise to be successful. Some school districts provide support for co-teaching models, and this is to be applauded. In addition, preservice teaching preparation programs need to include more instruction on effective co-teaching skills and models.

Teachers develop leadership skills that enable them to become a resource in their schools. In school districts across the United States, English language teachers have seen a change in their role in K–12 classrooms. They are increasingly called upon to provide professional development and/or act as coaches to peers in their school buildings (Staehr Fenner, 2016). The skills required for working with adults are different from those needed for working with children. It cannot be assumed that all English language teachers are prepared for this changing role. Nevertheless, we need to develop the professional leadership skills necessary for this new role. The *Standards for TESOL Pre-K–12 Teacher Preparation Programs* (TESOL International Association, 2018) is an excellent source for learning about our new professionalism.

A Look Back and a Look Ahead

The 6 Principles that Chapter 3 describes are the basic tenets that guide our profession. Some of these principles may overlap with the guidelines for other professionals in K–12 contexts. Taken as a whole, however, they outline the distinctive responsibilities and skills of all professionals who teach English learners. They concisely state what exemplary teaching of English learners requires teachers to do:

Principle 1. **Know Your Learners.** Teachers gather information about each student's background, particularly those aspects that are consequential for their language development. These aspects include learners' native languages and cultures, their levels of English language development, and all the factors that can support or hinder their second language development.

Principle 2. **Create Conditions for Language Learning.** Teachers make their classrooms into spaces where students are motivated to learn, practice, and take risks with language. Teachers work to secure all the essential conditions of second language acquisition, draw on beneficial conditions, and set high expectations for their learners.

Principle 3. **Design High Quality Lessons for Language Development.** Teachers know what students can do at their current level of language development and what they need to learn next. Then teachers determine lesson objectives, plan how they will convey content information, promote rich classroom conversations, decide on tasks that are meaningful and encourage authentic language practice, and explicitly teach learning strategies and critical thinking skills.

Principle 4. **Adapt Lesson Delivery as Needed.** Teachers monitor their students' comprehension, adjusting teacher talk or materials, differentiating instruction, and scaffolding tasks according to students' English language proficiency levels. In short, effective teaching of English learners requires decision-making during the lesson delivery on the basis of student responses and actions and a solid understanding of the second language development process.

Principle 5. **Monitor and Assess Student Language Development.** Teachers gauge how well students are making progress in academic English, note and evaluate the types of errors that students make, offer strategic feedback, and use a variety of assessment types to measure student achievement.

Principle 6. **Engage and Collaborate within a Community of Practice.** Teachers understand that they can serve English learners better when they work together. Teaching English learners requires that teachers be part of a community of practice within their school and the broader education community that affords them access to ongoing professional development. Teachers should co-plan with colleagues so they understand the language and content demands of each subject that a learner studies.

Each of the 6 Principles challenges teachers of English learners to develop professionally. Appendix B provides a self-assessment checklist for teachers to use to evaluate their own implementation of the 6 Principles and supporting practices. Our school systems are changing rapidly, our students are increasingly diverse, and, as professionals, we must also change and grow while holding fast to those principles that we know will lead to excellence and achievement for our learners.

Chapter 4 builds on the practices described in Principle 6 and highlights the ways in which teachers of English learners can be resources for other educators in their schools and districts. The chapter moves beyond this particular function to explain how English language teachers can be agents of change, advocating for their students and acting as liaisons among families, school personnel, and the community.

Additional resources pertaining to this chapter are available at www.the6principles.org/K-12.

4 ADDITIONAL ROLES FOR TEACHERS OF ENGLISH LEARNERS

I graduated from college as a Spanish major and taught high school Spanish for several years. During that time, many families from different countries moved into the neighborhood where I was teaching. We didn't have ESL classes at the time, but the principal asked me to form a class with the ten English learners in the school. "You teach language, so you should be able to figure out how to teach them," he said. Well, I didn't know very much about teaching these students, but I loved trying! This experience inspired me to go back to school to get my TESOL degree. It seemed like a simple transition from teaching Spanish to teaching English; I didn't realize at the time that teaching English learners was much more than teaching a content area. On the contrary, it involved a whole slew of other responsibilities, each more demanding yet at the same time more rewarding than the next.

ESL/ELD, bilingual, and dual language teachers (subsequently, "English language teachers," for brevity) come to the profession by many different pathways. Some were English learners (ELs) themselves and want to help others learn English. Some have an interest in other cultures or languages and want to work with immigrant communities. Still others, like the teacher in the vignette above, were originally teachers of other academic subjects but then developed an interest in working with English learners. When they do so, they are often struck by the many and varied roles that teachers of English learners assume outside the classroom.

But even if elementary grade-level, secondary content, and special education teachers are not certified ESL/ELD teachers, they are in fact teachers of English learners if they have English learners in their classrooms. English learners succeed academically when all staff in the school community take responsibility for educating, assisting, mentoring, and guiding them in various ways (National Education Association, 2015). Therefore, this chapter is applicable to *all teachers* who have English learners in their classrooms.

Being a teacher of English learners involves being a mentor and counselor to these students and a resource to other staff who may have recently received English learners in their classrooms. Teachers of English learners are also an important link to parents or guardians of ELs, and as such, they serve as advocates for these students and their families. They play a vital role on school leadership teams and committees, and they often become involved in curriculum writing and textbook decisions. Even though these extra roles increase their workload several times over, many take them on with passion and commitment in order to provide a successful educational experience for their students.

When they assume these varied roles, teachers of English learners often become agents of change in their school districts. As they interact with colleagues and administrators by participating in meetings, on committees, and through informal dialogue, they communicate information about their students and share effective strategies for teaching them. They advocate for the resources and services that students need to succeed in school and graduate. They point out that the label "English learner" represents a temporary status. Most EL students can and do graduate from high school, and many go on to college and successful careers.

With the increase in academic rigor over the past two decades and the emergence of high-stakes testing and accountability, the knowledge and skills that teachers of English learners possess have become even more vital than ever before as schools search for strategies to increase their effectiveness with their students (Staehr Fenner, 2013). The sections that follow describe the various roles that teachers of English learners take on to promote the academic success of their students, and they detail these roles within the framework of the 6 Principles for exemplary teaching of English learners.

Mentor or Counselor

Supporting Principle 1. *Know Your Learners*

Find out what concerns your learners have and how you can help.

At some point in their careers, effective teachers of all grades and subjects play the role of mentor or counselor to particular students. For teachers of English learners, however, these roles are customary. Many families of our English learners arrive in the United States with minimal knowledge of U.S. schools or the ways in which U.S. school districts function. Teachers of English learners often become the "go to" staff person that the student and parents or guardians communicate with, trust, and rely on for information and advice. Because teachers of English learners are experienced at working with these learners and their families, they can find ways to communicate, even if they don't speak their students' home languages. Because they are used to dealing with students and families new to this country, they can often anticipate their questions and needs, and our students find it easy to approach them with issues and concerns.

Some English learners have come to this country to escape violence, poverty, or a natural disaster, and in the United States they may end up living with a relative whom they have not seen in many years or whom they have not even met. After the disastrous earthquake in Haiti in 2010, for example, several districts received many Haitian students, some of whom had lost one or both parents in the tragedy. In the vignette below, a teacher of English learners at a middle school shares the experience of a student who entered his class shortly after the earthquake.

> My student, Jean, was living in Haiti when the earthquake struck. Fortunately, his immediate family was spared, but they couldn't find his aunt, who lived in the same neighborhood in Port-au-Prince. They heard that she hadn't been at home during the earthquake, so they hoped that she was still alive somewhere. They searched all over but couldn't find her. They remained optimistic that she would turn up. Sadly, when they reached the rubble of her home, rescuers were just lifting her crushed body from the debris. Jean was in tears when he told me the story, and he ate lunch with me in my classroom every day after that.

In such sensitive cases, English learners may see their English language teacher or any of their teachers as an anchor in an otherwise chaotic and frightening transition to a new life. The stability offered by schools in general, and a special teacher in particular, is critical as students struggle through transition and adjustment.

Advocate

Supporting Principle 2. *Create Conditions for Language Learning*

Promote appropriate academic programs and services and a safe and welcoming environment for students and families.

As advocates, teachers of English learners strive to ensure that students receive an "equitable and excellent education by taking appropriate actions on their behalf" (Staehr Fenner, 2014, p. 8). Both the National Board for Professional Teaching Standards (2016) and the *Standards for TESOL Pre-K–12 Teacher Preparation Programs* (TESOL International Association, 2018) see advocacy as a central role of the English language teacher. But with so many English learners now in our schools, the responsibility for advocacy has spread to all teachers of English learners (National Education Association, 2015). Unfortunately, the need for advocacy is great because many of our students confront barriers that may impede their success in school.

One such barrier is the under-preparation of teachers at preservice institutions. Some grade-level and content teachers, though well intentioned, may lack knowledge about second language acquisition and the academic needs of English learners, and consequently, may not be adequately prepared to teach them. As mentioned in Chapter 1, national standards for teacher education do not mandate that all preservice teachers complete significant coursework related to teaching English learners, yet many of these teachers have English learners in their classrooms. As a result, some teachers may not know which strategies and materials work best with English learners, and some may not have the same high expectations for English learners that they have for other students.

Another barrier is discrimination in the school and wider community, and this can affect English learners and their families in direct and subtle ways as they attempt to succeed academically, socially, emotionally, and financially in their new country. Teachers of English learners can help by providing a voice for students and their families who have not yet developed their own strong voice to advocate for themselves (Staehr Fenner, 2014). In light of the rapid growth in numbers of English learners in many locations in the United States (National Center for Education Statistics, 2017) and the persistent achievement gap, serving our students effectively and equitably requires that all teachers of English learners take specific steps to advocate for them. Advocates can provide a voice in five key areas:

- Academics
- Social and emotional needs
- Access to programs and opportunities
- Support for families
- Societal and legal issues

Academics

Supporting Principle 3. *Design High-Quality Lessons for Language Development*

Before the No Child Left Behind Act of 2001, many districts across the country assumed that the education of English learners was mainly the responsibility of the English language teacher. This legislation, although problematic in some respects (National Education Association, n.d.), put the progress of English learners on the national radar, and this higher visibility has been sustained in the subsequent federal education

> Encourage all teachers to learn appropriate techniques for educating English learners.

law, the Every Student Succeeds Act (ESSA), passed by Congress in 2015. Districts have to disaggregate and report the high-stakes testing scores of English learners annually. Because an achievement gap between English learners and non-English learners persists, schools have had to seek ways to improve the performance of their English learners. In many cases, district leaders turn to the English language teachers and administrators for help in improving the quality of education of English learners so that test scores will rise.

In most education settings however, English learners spend only part of their day with their English language teacher while spending many hours with grade-level teachers at the elementary level or content teachers at the secondary level. These grade-level and content teachers may need support and training to acquire the tools necessary to deliver appropriate instruction to English learners. As expressed in the vision outlined in Chapter 1, an important part of the work of teachers of English learners is to advocate for making their school a place where all teachers recognize that the education of English learners is a shared responsibility. In such a school, all staff learn approaches and best practices to make academic content accessible to all students and work together to promote the development of academic English (Horwitz et al., 2009; Staehr Fenner, 2014). At the secondary level, teachers of English learners also advocate for these students to have appropriate courses and pathways that lead to graduation.

In districts where English learners do spend most of their day with their English language teachers, as in some newcomer programs, educators must recognize that this type of schedule is short term, in place only until the students have some knowledge of English. Just as with any student in the district, English learners are entitled to be educated by teachers who are qualified and certified in their respective subjects—but these teachers must have the skills necessary to educate English learners effectively.

Teachers of English learners can encourage all staff in their schools to be aware of and sensitive to the various cultures of their students so that they may use this information to interact more effectively and with greater understanding with students and their families. In addition, they can help colleagues understand the importance of students' maintaining and even improving their home language, since facility with the home language helps promote English proficiency (Genesee, n.d.). The ability to use the home language can also be an asset in the future as students go on to college and careers (Commission on Language Learning, 2017).

All teachers can advocate for programs in their districts that help English learners maintain and improve proficiency in their home language, such as dual language programs (Thomas & Collier, 2003) and native language arts classes (for example, Spanish for Native Speakers). They can encourage school libraries to have an adequate supply of books in students' home languages. In recent years, many states and districts have developed a "Seal of Biliteracy" to be embossed on students' high school diplomas, indicating that they have succeeded in becoming proficient in English and another language—an accomplishment of which to be proud (see www.sealofbiliteracy.org).

Social and Emotional Needs

Supporting Principle 1. *Know Your Learners*

Help learners get the assistance they need to overcome difficult circumstances

Mario, age 16, left Honduras in a hurry, taking his little sister with him. He had stopped going to school after third grade because gangs were kidnapping students and threatening to kill them if they didn't join. But the situation had recently gotten worse, and Mario feared for his sister's life and his own. He and his sister crossed the U.S. border in Texas, and after three months in a detention center, they ended up living with their brother, whom they had not seen for many years and hardly knew. Mario and his sister now go to school. Mario's classes are very hard for him; his sister is doing a little better. After school, Mario rushes off to his dishwashing job to earn money that he and his sister can live on. He wants to stay in school and graduate, but he is only in ninth grade and is having trouble trying to work long hours and pass his subjects in school.

As teachers of English learners know, many of our students come to school with social, emotional, and financial issues that are beyond those that are part of a child's typical experience or development. English learners may have left a war-torn country or experienced violence or extreme poverty. Some have been victims of religious persecution or witnessed a relative being arrested or killed. Others have arrived in the United States to live with a parent or relative whom they hardly know (Custodio & O'Loughlin, 2017).

A promising program developed to address the emotional needs of students who come to school in the United States having experienced trauma is Cognitive Behavioral Intervention for Trauma in Schools (CBITS). Staff members with counseling backgrounds or clinicians from outside agencies are trained to run group sessions with students who need support in order to function in the school setting. (More information about CBITS can be found at https://cbitsprogram.org/.)

Even if English learners have arrived in the United States with an intact family or were born in this country, they may experience a clash of cultures if their American friends live by one set of rules but their immigrant parents insist on a different set. These circumstances can cause turmoil in children and adolescents as they grow up, and they may need counseling services to work through these issues. Teachers of English learners can advocate for appropriate counseling services to be available, both in the school setting and outside school, and in the student's home language, if needed. Teachers can stay informed about developments around the country and the world that can affect the educational, social, and emotional well-being of English learners.

Access to Programs and Opportunities

Supporting Principle 6. *Engage and Collaborate within a Community of Practice*

Most school districts support the needs and interests of their students by offering distinct programs such as special education and gifted and talented services. Programs may be available in the arts, sciences, languages, or sports. Unfortunately, often, English learners do not have access to these valuable opportunities, nor do they know how to gain access. Sometimes students (and their parents or guardians) simply are not aware that these opportunities exist. Because of the language barrier, students may not hear an announcement at school, or their parents may not understand a notice that was sent home. In other cases, school staff may not believe that English learners have the ability to participate, since they may wrongly assume that determining their talents or needs will be difficult because they have low proficiency in English.

> Work with your colleagues to ensure that all programs and opportunities are accessible to English learners.

Teachers of English learners can work to ensure that our students have access to the programs that they may need for success or may want for enrichment or enjoyment. This is especially important in the area of special education, where English learners may be denied services for years while districts wait until students learn enough English to be tested with common testing instruments. Even if students are not yet fluent in English, there are other ways to determine whether they have special needs that can be addressed through appropriate services. By the same token, it is equally important to ensure that English learners are not referred for special education simply because they have difficulty with English—that is, as a result of a language *difference* rather than a language *disability*. The federal government and several states have published guidance documents in this area (a list of these resources is available at www.colorincolorado.org /special-education-ell/resources).

Similarly, English learners may be denied the opportunity to participate in programs for students who are considered academically talented. Because screening for these programs may be conducted totally in English, English learners may have difficulty performing well, even if they possess the required knowledge or ability. As in the case of screening for special needs, teachers of English learners can advocate for school districts to use alternative methods, such as the Naglieri Nonverbal Ability Test, for determining whether a student who is not yet fluent in English is capable of participating in such programs (U.S. Department of Education & U.S. Department of Justice [USED & USDOJ], 2015). They should also advocate for teachers in these programs to use effective strategies to help English learners be successful.

Many English learners are talented in the arts or sports. Since participating in programs in the arts or on sports teams affords English learners valuable opportunities to interact and develop friendships with English-proficient students, teachers of English learners should encourage this involvement. These extracurricular activities provide an excellent opportunity for English learners to improve their skills, practice their English, and enjoy school.

Support for Families

Supporting Principle 6. *Engage and Collaborate within a Community of Practice*

Encourage the school district to have supports and services in place for families.

In one school district in Connecticut, potential English learners and their families new to the district are directed to the English Learner Welcome Center, where interpreters are available to welcome families and explain district procedures. At the center, students are screened for English language services and also assessed in home language literacy (when possible) and math. Parents or guardians are interviewed so that the district can obtain a full educational history of the students to help with program placement. The families are then assisted in filling out registration and free/reduced price lunch forms, and in obtaining health services. Before they leave the center, they are given a "welcome gift," which consists of a welcome letter, a city and bus map, a public library card application, a list of city services, and a gift for the student. Depending on the grade level, this gift could be a bilingual dictionary, a book, a set of alphabet flash cards, or a vocabulary game. The goal is for families to leave the center with their questions answered and a sense that the school district is happy to meet them and ready to welcome them into their new community.

When families move to a new town or city, they usually go through an adjustment period during which they must locate and establish access to many places and services such as schools, doctors, and child care. However, when the family does not yet speak English and comes from a different culture, the task of becoming familiar with their new surroundings can be daunting. In some locations, school districts may have established structures to assist families (e.g., welcome centers, parent liaisons), but in other situations, the teachers who receive the students may hear about difficulties that the students or families encounter as they try to navigate the school district's procedures, forms, and requirements. These teachers can advocate for structures and services to be in place and easily accessible to new families.

Teachers of English learners can ensure that when families arrive in the district, they are treated with respect and enter a welcoming atmosphere. If the school personnel who receive families are capable of assisting them in their home language, or if an interpreter can be available, in person or through technology, families will feel more at ease. Teachers of English learners can discuss the important advantages of such personnel with administrators. In addition, teachers of English learners can work with district or building staff to put procedures in place to help families gain access to needed school and community support services for themselves and their children. Teachers can develop contacts at local agencies so that they can call on them to help families in need. They can also encourage the district to offer ESL/ELD classes (and GED or citizenship classes, if appropriate) for adults so that family members can start on the road to empowerment and independence and can demonstrate to their children that they are learning English too.

Once a family becomes part of the school community, teachers of English learners can advocate for interpreters at school functions and especially at parent-teacher conferences so that parents can understand information about their children's progress and learn strategies for helping them at home. Because members of some families have multiple jobs and many responsibilities to keep track of, teachers can make phone calls home (with the assistance of interpreters, if needed) to remind parents of upcoming events at school and encourage them to attend. They can plan special functions, especially at the beginning of the school year, to explain the expectations and responsibilities of the family (such as providing children with a quiet place to study) and the services and assistance that the school can provide (such as special education, social work services, and interpreters at meetings). They can also plan a family literacy night or other events at which families have an opportunity to enjoy reading, writing, or craft activities organized around a theme, book, or author. (For ideas, see http://classroom.synonym.com/plan-family-literacy-night -school-4499292.html.) At these functions, teachers can also provide activities to help new families meet and get to know one another so that they can form their own support systems. (For more ideas about getting families involved, see www.adlit.org/article/42781/.)

Teachers of English learners can also advocate for the translation of school-home communication, report cards, district websites, and robocall scripts into the major languages of the school community. School and district handbooks, course selection guides, and other major district publications may also need to be translated. If certain legal or technical publications, such as special education mandates, are written with legal or educational jargon, teachers of English learners can encourage the district to use everyday language in the translations, especially if parents or guardians are unfamiliar with uch services or lack years of formal education. (For federal regulations regarding the obligations of school districts to provide interpretation and translations, see www.brycs.org/documents/upload/Interpretation-Translation-FAQ.pdf.)

Societal and Legal Issues

Supporting Principle 1. *Know Your Learners*

Three years ago at a local high school in the Northeast, the valedictorian was a former English learner. He had come to the United States from Mexico when he was eight years old, and he entered fourth grade in the district, not knowing any English. After a rough start and an adjustment period, it became evident that he was a bright and highly motivated student. By the eighth grade, he had exited the ESL/bilingual program, and by the time he graduated from high school, he had taken numerous Advanced Placement and other challenging courses, and he ended up with the highest grade-point average in the school. In his speech at graduation, he acknowledged the important role that his first ESL teacher had played in his education while she sat in the audience beaming as his special guest.

If your students are undocumented, educate your colleagues about the sensitive nature of this issue and the right of all students to an education.

The student had been accepted at an Ivy League university, and he very much wanted to attend. However, because of his undocumented status, he could not receive federal financial aid, and, without substantial financial help, he could not attend such an expensive university. He had also been accepted at the highest-ranked state university in the area. However, in keeping with state policy, that university did not offer financial aid to undocumented students. It gave him the option to attend, but only as an international student, paying costly out-of-state tuition. In the end, he decided to attend the local community college for his first year. Fortunately, after that year, the state changed its university tuition policy for undocumented students, and he was able to enroll at the state university and pay the in-state rate. He graduated with honors and is now pursuing a career in business.

The preceding vignette illustrates the financial and political challenges that some of our English learners face as they attempt to continue their education after high school. Many are denied opportunities for furthering their education because they cannot obtain the necessary funds from either educational or financial institutions as a result of their legal status. In some cases, students who arrived in the United States as children are not even aware of their undocumented status until they start to apply for college and financial aid. These students are often devastated to learn that they face major obstacles pursuing the career and life goals that they had so worked hard for and had hoped to accomplish.

Teachers of English learners can ensure that all staff know that even if students are undocumented, they have the same right to a K–12 education as all other students. It is important that staff be informed that when new families arrive at school, asking about immigration status or documentation of that status is, in fact, a violation of their civil rights (USED & USDOJ, 2014). Further, it is important to realize that even if an English learner was born in this country, one or both parents may be undocumented, and the family may be living in fear of deportation and separation. Teachers of English learners can watch for signs of anxiety and distress and seek support for the student and family.

Supporting Principle 6. *Engage and Collaborate within a Community of Practice*

Become informed, and actively support better educational opportunities for your students.

Teachers of English learners can get involved in advocating for English learners through various channels outside the classroom. They can support the passage of legislation and policies, such as an in-state college tuition policy, to help ELs extend their education beyond high school and allow them to work and be responsible, contributing members of society. Teachers can invite legislators into their classrooms to see the "face" of English learners, with the hope that lawmakers will become more sensitive to issues regarding our students and the need for funding to support various programs.

As noted in Chapter 3, teachers of English learners can join professional organizations to stay informed about issues concerning ELs. At the local level, they can attend school board meetings in their district to appeal for adequate funding for staffing, courses, and programs to help English learners succeed.

Resource for Colleagues

Although the number of English learners is rising rapidly in the United States, the preservice training of grade-level and content teachers who have English learners in their classrooms lags behind (Nutta, Mokhtari, & Strebel, 2012). As a result, many of these teachers need support to serve English learners when they start teaching in their school districts (McGraner & Saenz, 2009). Therefore, teachers of English learners have a major role to play in helping their colleagues work with English learners more effectively in their classrooms. The teachers who can serve in this way as resources to their colleagues could be the English language teachers, or they could be other teachers who have developed skills and expertise in teaching English learners. For example, a science teacher who has learned strategies for teaching English learners and has successfully taught a sheltered science class such as ESL Biology for several years will have much guidance to offer new science teachers who have English learners in their classrooms.

In addition, as discussed in the previous chapter, it is the responsibility of all teachers of English learners to keep abreast of the latest research and developments in the field of English language teaching by pursuing their own professional development. They can read professional articles and journals, attend conferences and workshops, and take online courses, among other ways to build knowledge and skills.

Professional Development Needs

Supporting Principle 3. *Design High-Quality Lessons for Language Development*

Teachers of English learners can help their colleagues gain the knowledge and skills necessary to feel confident and be successful with the English learners in their classrooms by providing professional development in the following general areas:

> Help your colleagues use effective strategies for teaching English learners in their classrooms.

- The process of second language acquisition (see Chapter 2) and ways that all teachers can promote it

- Cross-cultural communication and diversity sensitivity, as well as specific cultural information about the ethnolinguistic groups served by the school district

- Accommodations recommended for English learners on classroom, district, and state assessments, and information about additional state-mandated assessments that English learners take to measure language proficiency

- Strategies and techniques that integrate content and language instruction and allow English learners at all levels of English proficiency to have access to and participate in grade-level, standards-based instruction (see Chapter 3 for specific strategies). Because there are numerous techniques and ways to incorporate them into the existing curricula in various content areas, this topic for professional development needs significant attention and could be ongoing for an entire year or longer.

Delivering Professional Development

Supporting Principle 6. *Engage and Collaborate within a Community of Practice*

Last year I worked at an elementary school doing pull-out and push-in instruction for English learners. One of the grade 5 teachers, Mr. Romero, reported that the English learners in his class were having difficulty with math instruction, so we decided that I would push in during math time. I decided to use a co-teaching technique that I had heard about but had never tried. During the lesson, whenever I sensed that the English learners weren't getting it or needed more support, I would pretend that I didn't understand, and I would ask questions that I thought the students needed to ask. For example, when Mr. Romero was teaching about adding mixed numbers, such as $5\frac{3}{4} + 6\frac{1}{2}$, and I sensed that some of my students were confused, I said, "Oh, so, Mr. Romero, do you mean I have to change the $\frac{1}{2}$ to $\frac{3}{4}$ before I can add them together? And I do it like this?" Then I would demonstrate on the board how to do it. And then I would say, "Can I try another example on the board, just to make sure I understand?" I would continue this way throughout the lesson so that the English learners— and others—had more opportunities for practice. After a few days, I noticed that Mr. Romero began to slow his pace, build in more examples, and write on the board more often.

> Use various means to provide professional development for your colleagues.

In the preceding vignette, the ELD teacher demonstrated some effective practices through co-teaching. This is one strategy among many that teachers who have experience teaching English learners can use to impart ideas to and discuss them with colleagues. In so doing, they embody the belief that educating English learners is a shared responsibility, and teachers can learn from one another (Staehr Fenner, 2014).

The methods of professional development in use may depend on the structure and time allotted in the school or district and the personalities involved. Some approaches are more formal, such as a series of full-day workshops, whereas others can occur informally, as when two teachers sit down and talk at lunch once a week. Any means can be effective if teachers are open and willing to learn and improve their teaching practices. A combination of approaches may work best. Professional development suggestions follow:

- Presenting a workshop
- Presenting a "technique of the month" at faculty meetings
- Participating in grade-level or departmental meetings
- Joining professional learning communities (PLCs)
- Organizing "lunch and learn" sessions
- Observing and coaching or mentoring individual teachers
- Modeling a lesson or technique for colleagues
- Inviting grade-level or content teachers to observe ESL/ELD classes
- Co-teaching and demonstrating techniques and debriefing afterwards
- Establishing online communities for sharing ideas, techniques, and lesson plans
- Setting up opportunities for content teachers to shadow an English learner for an entire day. When teachers experience a school day through the eyes of English learners, they become more aware of their need for professional development to serve English learners better (Soto, 2012).

Professional development should be a two-way street. Just as English language teachers can help their colleagues understand the needs of English learners, so too can grade-level and content teachers assist them in understanding the tasks and assignments required of the students in their classrooms. With academic demands high, English language teachers can improve their instruction by adjusting their teaching to provide English learners with the prerequisite knowledge and skills for these content classrooms.

Other Ways to Assist Colleagues

Besides providing professional development, teachers of English learners can assist colleagues in many other areas for the benefit of our students. One way is to help English learners in the ESL/ELD classroom prepare for upcoming lessons in grade-level and content classrooms. ESL/ELD teachers can accomplish this by pre-teaching vocabulary, building background for upcoming lessons, or teaching reading and writing skills that will be needed. In addition, ESL/ELD teachers can review or reteach information in the ESL/ELD classroom that has already been taught in grade-level and content classrooms. ESL/ELD teachers can therefore address confusing concepts or clear up any misconceptions. Such collaboration among teachers takes coordination, but working together in this manner can have a positive effect on the academic outcomes of English learners (Honigsfeld & Dove, 2010).

ESL/ELD and other teachers with experience teaching English learners in their classes, can assist colleagues in important ways outside the classroom. Even though some of these actions are not explicit professional development, they are indirect ways of demonstrating effective practices that colleagues can begin to implement on their own. Such actions include the following:

- Helping with lesson planning by suggesting effective language development techniques
- Suggesting supplemental text materials, at various reading levels or in the home language (Baker et al., 2014; Echevarría, Vogt, & Short, 2017)
- Modifying classroom assessments to reduce the amount of language

- Identifying suitable instructional supports and testing accommodations, such as using bilingual glossaries, reading aloud test questions, and allowing extended time on assessments
- Helping colleagues interpret the results of English language proficiency assessments, as well as other state and local assessments
- Identifying key language forms and functions in written materials that need to be explained to students (Cloud, Genesee, & Hamayan, 2009; Short & Echevarría, 2016; Zwiers, 2008).
- Serving on Response to Intervention (RtI) and special education referral teams
- Helping colleagues understand the value of English learners' use of their home language to understand content
- At the secondary level: Meeting with guidance counselors to assist in determining the most appropriate programming and class schedules for English learners.

Developer and Reviewer of Curricula, Materials, and Assessments

Supporting Principle 3. *Design High-Quality Lessons for Language Development*

Even with the surge of English learners across the United States, quite often curriculum, materials, and assessments are designed without substantial consideration for the unique needs of English learners. A noteworthy example is the Common Core State Standards (CCSS; National Governors Association Center for Best Practices & Council of Chief State School Officers, 2010), which many states use to guide the instruction of English language arts, math, and literacy skills within other content areas. Although CCSS addresses foundational literacy skills and vocabulary in the standards for kindergarten and grade 1, these skills are not mentioned anywhere in the secondary school standards. Certainly, beginning English learners of all ages need to acquire those foundational skills. CCSS makes little mention of English learners anywhere and offers almost no guidance on using the standards with English learners.

> Assist in the development of curricula, materials, and assessments, which are the backbone of high-quality language lessons.

Some publishers do now consider English learners and consult with experts in the field when writing materials. These resources are helpful, and we hope to see more of them in the future. But a great deal of work remains to be done to make curricula, materials, and assessments appropriate for our English learners.

Teachers of English learners can help to improve curricula, materials, and assessments in several ways. At the state level, they can serve on curriculum development committees, helping to develop or revise English language frameworks or standards. They may participate in state-level efforts to infuse language development and English learner–appropriate teaching techniques into grade-level and content-area frameworks. At the district level, they can collaborate with district staff to write English language development curricula and infuse best practices for English learning into district curriculum frameworks, enabling all teachers to engage English learners in appropriate instruction in the core content areas.

Teachers of English learners may also design or review district formative and summative assessments or create rubrics for measuring student progress, taking into consideration the different English proficiency levels that students exhibit. They may also design or review textbooks, technology, or other teaching materials, print and digital, to ensure that they are responsive to the needs of English learners.

Participant on School and District Committees for Programming and Policy

Supporting Principle 6. *Engage and Collaborate within a Community of Practice*

Work together with your colleagues to develop or adjust programming and policies.

About three years ago, our school district began to get many "unaccompanied minors" who crossed the U.S. border in Texas and ended up in our community. Because most of them were students with limited or interrupted formal education (SLIFE), it became apparent quickly that we were not meeting their needs with our regular ESL sheltered high school courses. Our administrator called together a group of teachers of English learners, principals, and counselors to design an "International Academy" for these students, with new courses in basic literacy and basic math, and counseling services offered by a bilingual social worker. After about two years, however, we realized that we needed to do more. Most of these students were over-aged for their grades and needed to make money after school to support themselves and their families. Some of them were showing up late for school after arriving home after midnight from their jobs, and others skipped school altogether. They didn't see a direct connection between staying in school and their futures, and they had more immediate financial concerns. But we strongly believed that staying in school would help them in the long term, and we needed a hook to motivate them to keep up their attendance. We decided to build a career component into our program so that students could get training for realistic careers while they were pursuing their high school education. A group of us decided to form a committee to work on this new component, and we have sent out requests to local businesses to form partnerships.

With ESSA in effect nationwide, school districts across the United States have become more interested in ensuring that English learners' needs are taken into consideration when developing district policies and programs. The performance of English learners on high-stakes assessments and the graduation rate for ELs play a significant role in the rating of a school's and district's performance, so superintendents and other high-ranking officials are taking notice. They are looking to teachers of English learners and their administrators for insight and guidance as they review existing programming and policies or design new ones.

Teachers of English learners can serve on leadership teams to ensure that English learners' needs are considered in district and school improvement efforts. They may help design or refine academic programs for English learners as the population increases or student performance changes. For example, they may help design a newcomer program for older arrivals with limited formal schooling or a new writing intervention course for long-term English learners. They may encourage the establishment of an English learner tutoring center or an afterschool program in which students receive academic support. They may express the need for a welcome center, where English learners can be assessed for services while families receive information about various district policies regarding student behavior, homework, school buses, community services, and so forth. Teachers of English learners may also serve on policy committees of a more general nature so that the English learners' voices are heard across all ranges of district issues.

A Look Back and a Look Ahead

Chapter 4 examines the various roles and responsibilities of all teachers of English learners: ESL/ELD, bilingual, and dual language teachers; grade-level teachers at the elementary level; content teachers at the secondary level; special education teachers; and more. As detailed in the chapter, teachers of English learners serve as

- mentors or counselors for the students and their families to help them become familiar with the school system and their new community;

- advocates for the learners in several key areas: promoting learners' academic achievement, meeting their social and emotional needs, ensuring their access to programs and opportunities, supporting their families, and addressing societal and legal issues that they face;

- resources for colleagues, providing professional development, collaborating on lesson planning, identifying instructional supports and testing accommodations, helping select appropriate and/or supplemental materials, interpreting assessment results, and advising on programming for secondary English learners;

- participants on development teams for curricula, materials, and locally designed assessments and on leadership teams at their school sites.

As teachers take on these various roles, they become agents for change that can have many positive effects on the education of English learners. Although these extra responsibilities are considerable and time-consuming, teachers of English learners find great satisfaction in knowing that they are making a difference in the lives of our students.

Teachers of English learners cannot meet all the needs of ELs on their own. In sharing their expertise with colleagues, they help build capacity within their school, but offering a truly exemplary education to English learners requires the engagement of *all educators* in the design and implementation of successful programs. Chapter 5 discusses the responsibilities of other professionals, both site-based and district-based, who play vital roles in the education of English learners.

Additional resources pertaining to this chapter are available at www.the6principles.org/K-12.

5 ESTABLISHING A CULTURE OF SHARED RESPONSIBILITY

uccessful schools for English learners have a shared sense of community and responsibility. Indeed, many school-based professionals support the education of English learners, not just classroom-based personnel. Reading specialists, instructional coaches, guidance counselors, and school and district administrators directly contribute to the overall success of programs and services designed for English learners. This chapter addresses those in key roles, while encouraging additional sharing with other personnel who interact with English learners and their families—from school nurses to security guards to cafeteria workers. Because key school-based professionals closely support the type of exemplary teaching that this book describes, these professionals are the focus of this chapter, which extends the discussion of the 6 Principles to outline how those beyond the classroom can further the implementation of exemplary programs in very meaningful ways. Not every principle is relevant for every group of educators, so this chapter examines only those that apply most directly to each group.

Chapter 5 provides recommendations for the following groups:

- Principals and assistant principals
- District curriculum directors
- Special education directors and gifted and talented program directors
- Reading specialists and instructional coaches
- Librarians and media specialists
- Guidance counselors, social workers, and school psychologists

The roles played by these groups are explored in different sections in the chapter. Taken together, these roles provide a full picture of a culture of shared responsibility for English learners in K–12 schools. If you are a member of one (or more) of these groups, you can "zoom in" on your own part and examine the recommendations for your role. If you find that you lack information or skills pertaining to any of the points presented, you can work to build those competencies and strengthen your practice so that you can fully contribute to the education of English learners. Many resources are provided in this book to help you do just that. To form a successful "community of practice" serving English learners and their families, all members must fulfill their respective roles effectively.

Community of practice, a term coined by Lave and Wenger in 1991, describes a group of individuals who engage in a process of collective learning as they practice their profession. These practitioners, each with his or her own skill set, join together to actively share knowledge, resources, experiences, and orientations to their work. They also build relationships that enhance their collaborative efforts. Certainly school-based practitioners are a community of practice. As a community with shared responsibility for all learners in the school, school-based practitioners can collectively move their school forward to ensure an equitable, high-quality education for English learners and can create a responsive school for their parents and guardians (Theoharis & O'Toole, 2011).

Each professional can advance her or his own knowledge and skills in working with or supporting those who work with English learners. Doing so furthers the mission of the entire school or district in continuously improving services for the learners and their families. Each can also work to be an effective member of his or her community of practice by establishing small learning communities and developing a shared vision and clear goals for the education of English learners in order to fully realize the 6 Principles for exemplary teaching of English learners.

If you or any of your colleagues do not feel ready to engage in any of the actions listed in this chapter, you can make learning about English learners a professional goal. Reach out to local colleges and universities, attend TESOL or TESOL affiliate conferences, join the Elementary, Secondary or Bilingual interest sections of TESOL, join online communities focused on English learner education, participate in online courses, or explore websites such as Colorín Colorado (www.colorincolorado.org) designed for teachers of English learners. You might also organize a book study group to foster the growth and development of all the professionals that make up your community of practice.

If you are a teacher of English learners or an English learner program director, you can move your school or district forward by sharing the appropriate sections of this chapter with your colleagues. This chapter addresses each group of educators in turn, yet it can also support school improvement teams and district- or site-based leaders as they work together to review their current programs and services for English learners and their families with an eye to school and program improvement (Movit, Petrykowska, & Woodruff, 2010). You can also offer to participate in schoolwide or districtwide committees formed to improve programs and services for English learners and their families.

School Principals and Assistant Principals

Making the School a Welcoming Place

As a new principal in an urban elementary school, Mrs. McArthur believed in the power of home visits to build strong relationships between teachers and families. But she recognized that many of her families spoke languages other than English at home and that if she decided to encourage her teachers to make home visits prior to the start of the school year, she would have to provide the support they would need. So first she reviewed the home language surveys conducted over the past two years. She could easily see the predominant languages of her school community. Next, she worked with support staff to identify speakers of those languages among her teachers, staff, and parent volunteers. Together, they planned the visits, forming teams as needed and discussing the welcoming message they wanted to give their families. They also discussed how they would handle the two languages when visiting to make sure that teachers and parents were at the center of the conversations. Finally, they reviewed important cultural differences in communication styles and culturally appropriate ways of interacting when visiting homes of families from each cultural community. Mrs. McArthur joined in the visits, concentrating on newly arrived refugee, immigrant, and migrant families to give them a special welcome. As a result of this effort, staff reported that the start of the next school year felt more positive. Teachers and parents were already comfortable with one another, and the result was increased participation by parents in the life of the school.

It is hard to overstate the critical role that school principals and assistant principals play as instructional leaders for their schools, especially when it comes to the delivery of a high-quality education to English learners. If you are a principal or assistant principal, you need substantial knowledge about English learners as well as the best instructional programs and research-based practices to serve them. You supervise and support classroom teachers serving English learners and need to be able to judge the quality of instruction going on in your school. In addition, you help guide the work of ancillary personnel, such as school guidance staff, librarians, reading specialists, and instructional coaches, and you need to ensure that they interact with English learners and their families effectively. You can turn to ESL/ELD, bilingual, and dual language teachers or program administrators (for brevity, subsequently identified as "English language teachers" or "English language specialists," as appropriate). Certainly, you will want to seek the advice of experts as you make decisions about improvements needed at your school in any aspect of program delivery. You can also work with English language specialists to make your school a welcoming place for families by establishing strong relationships with families from the cultural communities that make up your school.

This section is designed to guide you as you perform your critical role as instructional leader. Without your active involvement, your school is far less likely to fully realize the 6 Principles for exemplary teaching of English learners. Because this is so, we consider the 6 Principles in relation to your essential leadership role and detail actions that you can take to support those that are closely related to it.

Supporting Principle 1. *Know Your Learners*

- Get to know your school's families through home visits. You may join in making these visits, or you may encourage teachers or other school personnel to do so. By meeting families away from school, such as in community centers or in their homes, you may have more success in engaging families (Louie & Knuth, 2016).

- Before any home visits to families are carried out, ensure that all staff members are sensitive toward and skilled in interacting with families from the cultural communities represented in your school. "Conducting Home Visits" offers guidance to school-based personnel who aim to learn about the languages, cultures, educational backgrounds, and life experiences of their school's families. Gathering this information pays big dividends. It allows schools to gear up, assembling the resources—both material and human—that they need to serve their families well. It creates truly responsive schools, and this in turn enhances professional and parental satisfaction and student success (Gonzalez, Moll, & Amanti, 2005; Louie & Knuth, 2016; Stepanek & Raphael, 2010).

- Make sure that all staff members who interact with English learners and their families learn about, acknowledge, and affirm the strengths, capabilities, and contributions made by English learners and their families to your school. Ensure that students and families are not viewed from a deficit perspective (because *they don't know English yet*"). Instead, affirm the value that they add to the teaching/learning community because of the linguistic and cultural resources that they bring to the school. Be sure to consistently highlight the positive contributions and enrichment opportunities that English learners and their families make to your school community.

- Set a respectful and affirming tone by the way that you interact with culturally and linguistically diverse families.

- If your school has access to parent liaisons who have been hired to support the students and families participating in English learner programs, take full advantage of the special knowledge and skills that they bring to strengthen interactions between school and home.

Conducting Home Visits

- Learn all you can about the cultures of your families and the communities in which they live. Be sensitive to the cultural norms and behavioral expectations that make home-school interactions successful and comfortable. Family liaisons who work in your school's or district's English learner programs are an invaluable resource for this purpose.

- Conduct interviews or surveys in your families' home languages when the families first enroll their child in your school. Be sure to ask questions carefully, so that you learn accurate and detailed information about your families. Be mindful of the fact that norms of disclosure vary across cultures, making some questions feel inappropriate or too personal to some groups while not to others. Avoid asking questions that families will view as intrusive, and, before you begin, make sure that parents know the purpose of your questions and what you intend to do with the information.

- Inquire about the language or languages in which families would like to receive information from the school and whether they would prefer to receive information orally or in writing. Find out their preferred communication mode—printed material, phone, text message, or email. Try to determine the literacy level of parents by inquiring about the level of education that they were able to complete, so that you can be sure you are communicating effectively with your families.

- Learn the names of family members and how to pronounce them accurately.

- Learn about parents' expectations for their child's schooling, the expectations that parents have for teachers and the school, and the culturally determined roles that parents typically play in their child's education. Share this information so that all school personnel understand the many traditional roles that parents play in the education of their children from a cross-cultural perspective.

- Ask the parents to list or orally identify some strengths and interests that their child has, and pass this information on to the child's teacher(s).

- Find out ways in which the school can support families, and vice versa, and the types of community resources that parents may find valuable.

Sources: Gonzalez, Moll, & Amanti, 2005; Louie & Knuth, 2016; Stepanek & Raphael, 2010

Supporting Principle 2. *Create Conditions for Language Learning*

When Too Many Children Are Receiving Intervention

In a rural elementary school, Mr. Simoes, the school's principal, noticed that a high percentage of kindergarten and first-grade English learners were receiving intensive interventions in reading. When he checked into the situation, he was told that these students weren't meeting benchmarks and that was the reason they were all in the intervention program. Furthermore, he learned that they weren't making much progress despite the interventions that they were receiving. He learned that many students were being taught with a stand-alone phonics program created for students whose home language is English. He knew something had to be wrong if so many English learners were not meeting benchmarks and those receiving intensive intervention were not making good progress toward reading on grade level.

Mr. Simoes called a meeting of his school improvement team, making sure that the ESL teacher would be an essential member. He also contacted his local university to invite an ESOL reading specialist to participate. Mr. Simoes's hunch was right. The benchmarking tools and the benchmarks set were not appropriate for English learners. The team determined that the children had not been given sufficient time to learn to read in English before the benchmarks were applied in their

kindergarten and first-grade classes. The interventions being used also did not follow best prac-
tices regarding what leads to improved reading performance for English learners. As a result of
their discoveries, the team took corrective action and modified their assessment and intervention
systems to respond more appropriately to the learning characteristics and needs of their English
learners. Their first priority was to work together to make instruction in the regular classroom
more responsive to the students, but they also worked to establish more appropriate assessment
guidelines so that English learners would not be over-identified as needing intensive intervention.

- Create a welcoming environment for families and children at your school so that they feel a sense of belonging that supports learning. Make multilingualism the norm in signage in the halls, language abilities of front office staff, design of the school website, and all correspondence and communication with families. You may want to use multilingual communication text messaging technology such as Talking Points (www.talkingpts.org/) to facilitate cross-lingual communication among your staff and families.

- Ensure that all staff members are aware of the critical role played by the home language in second language learning and in learning in general. Make sure that students and families know that the school values their home language and welcomes it at school (Genesee & Lindholm-Leary, 2012). Support the use and the development of students' home languages to promote bilingualism and biliteracy leading to a "Seal of Biliteracy," if offered by your state. (See www.sealofbiliteracy.org/)

- Ensure that intake and enrollment procedures are easy to implement across the languages of the school. Create accessible information for parents, such as booklets or short videos in the home languages of the school community, to explain programmatic options and choices parents can make for their children.

- Hire teachers who have an ESL/ELD endorsement and staff who are multilingual and culturally sensitive; provide bilingual translators and interpreters for all parent meetings. "Best Practices in Working with Translators and Interpreters" offers further information on this topic. Take full advantage of the special knowledge and skills of parent liaisons who routinely interact with English learners and their families.

- Notice teaching and support staff members who might lack experience in working with English learners and give them professional development opportunities to grow and develop in this important area. As your English learner population changes, offer staff development to your instructional and support staff to help them understand and respond to important population shifts in your region.

- Encourage parents to take leadership or governance roles in the school and to work with school personnel to advocate for the needs of English learners with decision makers such as the school board, city council members, or state legislators.

- Protect the rights of English learners and their families. Ensure that you are well versed about the legal rights and relevant legislation governing the education of English learners, so that you can protect the rights and fulfill your responsibilities to English learners and their families.

- If you are not already familiar with the district plan for English learners, acquaint yourself with it and the common English learner program models in use (see Appendix A). As needed, work with others to develop additional programs that may be required to meet the needs of all English learners, including students with interrupted formal education, long-term English learners, new arrivals, and English learners with identified disabilities, so that all English learners can succeed.

- As you visit classrooms, evaluate the teaching and learning environments with respect to their cultural responsiveness, attending particularly to the use of time, space, instructional materials, student grouping arrangements, and conditions for testing.

Best Practices in Working with Translators and Interpreters

Bridging Refugee Youth & Children's Services (BYCS), *Interpretation/Translation in the Schools* (n.d.), www.brycs.org/clearinghouse/Highlighted-Resources-Interpretation-and-Translation-in-the-Schools.cfm

Minnesota Department of Education, *Working with Interpreters and Translators* (2009), https://education.state.mn.us/mdeprod/idcplg?IdcService=GET_FILE&dDocName=055113 &RevisionSelectionMethod=latestReleased&Rendition=primary

Australian Psychological Association, *Working with Interpreters: A Practice Guide for Psychologists* (2013), www.mhima.org.au/pdfs/APS-Working-with-Interpreters-Practice-Guide-for-Psychologists2013.pdf

American Speech-Language-Hearing Association, *Collaborating with Interpreters*, www.asha.org/PRPSpecificTopic.aspx?folderid=8589935334&section=Key_Issues.

Supporting Principle 3. *Design High-Quality Lessons for Language Development*

- To fully embrace your position as educational leader of your school, review all the chapters in this volume so that you are well versed in what constitutes a high-quality instructional program for English learners.
- Learn what good instruction for English learners looks like in a variety of classrooms—both stand-alone language development classes and sheltered content area classes (Short, Vogt, & Echevarría, 2017).[1] Ensure that lessons provide multiple entry points and are differentiated for students of varied language proficiency levels.
- Provide teachers with budgets to purchase materials (instructional and supplemental) that help meet the needs of diverse student populations, such as materials for grade-level curriculum units at accessible reading levels.
- For those working in collaborative classrooms, ensure that teachers are well prepared for their co-teaching roles, have joint planning time, and have the administrative support required to ensure their success (Honigsfeld & Dove, 2010).
- Promote interdisciplinary collaboration among teacher teams so that lessons are content-rich and provide the conditions needed for language learning.
- Set up workshops and other professional development opportunities to build staff competence in designing differentiated lessons for English learners—lessons that not only teach content but aid students in progressing to the next level of language proficiency.

---

[1] These classes have various names like ESL 1, content-based ESL, integrated ELD, sheltered biology, and structured English immersion.

Data Analysis for Program Improvement and Student Success

Ms. Rodriguez, the principal of a large urban middle school, and Mr. Sanchez, her assistant principal in charge of curriculum and instruction, meet each year to review the available student achievement data, looking for patterns and chances to make improvements for specific populations who attend their school. When it comes to their English learners, they know that it is important to disaggregate the data in many ways: by proficiency level, by ethnolinguistic background, by length of time in the program, by amount of previous schooling, and so forth. At the end of the last school year, when they looked at the available data, they clearly saw that a group of students who had been enrolled in English learner programs for six years or more had not yet exited the program and also were not faring well in educational achievement on statewide assessments. They took this as a call to action, meeting with the School Improvement Team, composed of school administrators, English language and reading specialists, parent liaisons, instructional coaches, and the district curriculum director. Together, they analyzed all plausible reasons for the pattern they were seeing, and they also surveyed the teachers serving these long-term English learners—particularly those who had ESL or bilingual certification and knew the students well.

Having done this, they wondered whether the standard ESL curriculum was really meeting these learners' needs. They saw a clear pattern of performance on language proficiency measures in which academic listening and writing were the lowest skills, and speaking and reading were the highest. Then they looked at the skills being emphasized in their curriculum. They determined that the curriculum was weak in the same areas in which they students were experiencing difficulty. That was their "Aha!" moment. Over the summer, they pulled together a team of English language and writing specialists to develop an ESL bridge course for only this group of students. They ensured that it focused on academic listening and writing. The course is being delivered to the students for the first time this year, so they will check in with the teachers and look at the data again at the end of the school year to make sure that the course is building the needed skills and leading to increased student success.

Because of federal legislation like the Every Student Succeeds Act (ESSA, 2015), which makes growth in English language proficiency a required indicator in state accountability systems, school-based leaders need to actively monitor student language development to make sure that students are progressing and that their English learner programs are working. A number of actions can assist school-based leaders in monitoring and ensuring the effectiveness of their programs:

- Make sure that all staff members understand the importance of growth in English language learning as part of the school's accountability targets.

- Make sure that all staff members are familiar with the English language proficiency tests used by your state and understand how to interpret and use the scores for planning instruction and assessment while considering students' proficiency levels by skill area (listening, speaking, reading, writing) and their length of time in the language support program.

- Ensure that all staff members who are responsible for the English language proficiency assessments have the preparation that they need to administer and interpret them. Provide sufficient time to administer the assessments with as little interruption to the instructional program as possible.

- Plan for teachers to use interim language proficiency assessments that are tied to the state's language proficiency system to monitor student progress in the four domains of language development—listening, speaking, reading, and writing—periodically during the school year.

- Use data generated from your English learner programs to improve program delivery to students. Disaggregate language proficiency and achievement data by subgroup, using achievement data known to be valid and reliable for English learners. Subgroups might include recent arrivals, long-term English learners, students with limited or interrupted formal education (SLIFE), or English learners with disabilities. In this way, you can identify unmet needs of particular groups of learners as well as brainstorm to develop solutions that will improve educational services and schooling conditions for the particular subgroups.

- If statewide or district assessments are required to be administered in English, exercise caution in interpreting scores for English learners who have only recently arrived or are at the lowest levels of English proficiency, to ensure that scores are interpreted fairly.

- Use formative assessment data as needed to provide a counter-narrative to statewide, standardized test results that may not adequately or accurately capture the success that your English learners are attaining. Share more student-responsive data sources with school board and city council members, state legislators, and the media to highlight the growth that you have documented in student performance with alternative measures.

- Ensure that instructional benchmarks and classroom assessments are appropriate for English learners, and consult specialists as needed when a pattern of under- or over-representation of English learners receiving intensive interventions or special services is detected.

- Ensure that all teachers know which accommodations their English learners are entitled to have on district and state assessments and offer them to students on district, statewide, and classroom-based assessments (Young, 2008).

Supporting Principle 6. *Engage and Collaborate within a Community of Practice*

- Consult TESOL experts, such as English language program administrators and teacher leaders from your district, teacher educators from local colleges and universities with TESOL and bilingual teacher education programs, and educational consultants with English language expertise, in the decision-making process for policies, curricula, and program development in your school. Involve them in all school committees.

- Develop your community of practice by creating a climate of respect for all staff, especially valuing the role of the ESL/ELD and bilingual specialists in the school.

- Build joint planning time into the school schedule for teachers who share English learners. Ensure that all personnel serving a given student are consulted and involved in all instructional and programmatic decisions affecting that student; also ensure that they are offering well-orchestrated instruction that is aligned in pedagogical approach and philosophy.

- Create access to community services for English learners and their families.

- Engage parents in meaningful ways; reduce barriers to parental involvement and provide opportunities for families to contribute to the life and direction of the school.

- Consult the English language teachers at all stages of the student referral process for an English learner who may have special learning needs. Make sure that at least one of these teachers is on the eligibility and IEP teams.

District Curriculum Directors

District curriculum directors make many curricular and instructional decisions that affect learners every day in classrooms, most often in conjunction with committees of dedicated and knowledgeable teachers and subject-matter specialists. However, while some instructional or supervisory personnel may be superb content experts, they may be less familiar with the needs of English learners or how to create a curriculum that is truly accessible for students new to English and, in many cases, new to U.S. curricula. If you are a curriculum director, you have a very important role to play in ensuring that all curricula that are adopted by your district are truly accessible by English learners of all proficiency levels and supports their educational success. The following are some of the actions that you can take to support the 6 Principles within a culture of shared responsibility for English learners in your district.

Supporting Principle 1. *Know Your Learners*

- Make sure that knowledge about teaching linguistically and culturally diverse students is evident in all district curricula. In particular, ensure that students of all proficiency levels can access district curricula, because these will suggest materials and strategies explicitly designed for English learners of varied proficiency levels—beginners to advanced.

- Look closely at the curricula taught in the district to make sure that they are appropriate for English learners, not only by affording multiple entry points as suggested above but also by empowering students through the use of themes and materials that connect well with the background knowledge, cultures, and life experiences that English learners bring to the classroom.

- If the district has a considerable number of students with interrupted or limited formal schooling, work with English language specialists to develop or adapt curricula to help them catch up academically with grade-level peers, while building needed literacy skills.

- Work to make sure that mandated curricular materials are readily available in the high-incidence home languages of your district, thus supporting delivery of the curricula in dual language and bilingual education programs, as well as providing readily accessible subject-matter materials for students who are literate in their home languages. This will allow students to learn valued content in their home or target language in addition to English.

Supporting Principle 2. *Create Conditions for Language Development*

- Work with school librarians and media specialists to build classroom and school library collections that are meaningful and relevant to English learners and list these in district curriculum guides. Find materials that match the proficiency levels of students in English, thus increasing their access to the district curricula.

- Build dual language and home language collections to support learning related to grade-level curricula for use at school and at home.

Supporting Principle 3. *Design High-Quality Lessons for Language Development*

- Make sure that all content-area curricula identify not only content objectives but also a range of language objectives that teachers can draw from when implementing the curriculum with English learners of various proficiency levels. Be sure to include language forms and structures, not just vocabulary, as language targets.

- Review all curricula to identify cultural or linguistic barriers that can impede the performance of English learners. Suggest ways to modify the curricula for English learners so that teachers take these into account in lesson delivery.
- Make sure that district curricula are aligned with and cross-reference the state English language proficiency standards—not just the state or national *content* standards—in order to aid teachers in aligning their lessons with all sets of standards that apply to English learners.

Supporting Principle 4. *Adapt Lesson Delivery as Needed*

- Inspect curriculum guides to evaluate their appropriateness for students of varied language proficiency levels and literacy levels. Add or modify suggested teaching activities to tailor the curricula for all English learners, and include model lessons that show teachers how to include English learners when delivering instruction.
- In all district curriculum guides, suggest foundational background information that English learners may need before studying common U.S. curricular topics, particularly if they have lived or been educated outside the United States. For example, they may need an orientation to U.S. geography before studying U.S. history to understand the locations where historic events are taking place. Or they may need an orientation to the English measurement system before performing operations that assume that they know the liquid measurement of a pint or a quart.
- Periodically revisit existing curricula to ensure their responsiveness to current English learners, particularly if backgrounds or learning needs change. For example, if students arrive speaking languages new to the district, find materials in these home languages for the curricular units mandated by the district and make them available to students.

Supporting Principle 5. *Monitor and Assess Student Language Development*

- Provide clear instructions about when assessments must be conducted in English and when they can be administered in students' home languages. If unit assessments are to be conducted in English, specify the testing accommodations that should be used in the classroom and provided to students to make the assessments as fair and valid as possible.
- Recognize cultural and experiential bias in test items, test content, and test format (e.g., timed tests) on both statewide and local assessments (Young, 2008).
- Ensure that district-developed tests
  - measure what is being taught in the most valid and fair way possible;
  - measure all learning objectives established for English learners (language and content);
  - do not discriminate against certain linguistic or cultural groups (Educational Testing Service [ETS], 2009);
  - are designed for students of all language proficiency levels.
- Revisit and modify existing curricula if assessment results determine that changes are needed to improve the performance of English learners because as a group they are not performing to expectations.

Special Education Directors and
Gifted and Talented Program Directors

When English learners are identified as having special education needs or as qualifying to participate in programs for students with special gifts and talents, they do not cease to be English learners. On the contrary, if they are to succeed in their instructional programs, their needs as English learners must be respected just as much as their identified disability or their special gifts and talents. If you are a special education director or a director of gifted and talented programs, you play a vital role in recognizing students' unique learning characteristics and meeting both types of their learning needs. Actions that you can take to help these English learners succeed will support the implementation of the 6 Principles within a culture of shared professional responsibility.

Supporting Principle 1. *Know Your Learners*

- Ensure that Response to Intervention (RtI), Multi-Tiered Systems of Support (MTSS), and special education procedures account for the linguistic and cultural characteristics of learners, and make sure that instruction offered at each tier is built on research-based teaching approaches known to be effective with English learners (Burr, Haas, & Ferriere, 2015).

- Take a hard look at benchmarks set at each grade level and benchmarking tools used by your district to identify learners in need of more intensive support. Examine the benchmarks and tools to determine whether they are valid and reliable for second language learners. Maintain and review student data to see whether particular subgroups of students are being over- or under-identified by current procedures and make changes as needed.

- To comply with legal guidelines, take special care to ensure that linguistic and cultural differences are never mistaken for disabilities and that students with limited formal schooling are not being served in special education placements for lack of appropriate general education alternatives (U.S. Department of Education & U.S. Department of Justice [USED & USDOJ], 2015).

- Likewise, make sure that students' lack of proficiency in English is not a barrier to their participation in programs for students with special gifts and talents. Use assessments with low or no language demands, such as the Naglieri Nonverbal Ability Test, to determine whether English learners are eligible for gifted and talented opportunities.

- Make sure that an English language teacher is present during all meetings for English learners who are going through the referral process or being considered for participation in gifted and talented programs.

Supporting Principle 2. *Create Conditions for Language Learning*

- Make sure that all communication to parents is provided in the language they prefer and that only qualified interpreters are present during eligibility and IEP meetings. These steps can empower parents to advocate for their children's educational needs. (See "Best Practices in Working with Translators and Interpreters," on page 86.)

- Ensure that English learners with disabilities are afforded all the instructional accommodations to which they are entitled as English learners.

- Make sure that special educators understand how to shape instruction for students of various proficiency levels and that they know the current proficiency levels of their learners in listening, speaking, reading, and writing. Remember that, by law, dually identified students must receive both ESL and special education services (USED & USDOJ, 2015).

- Make sure that all programs are open and responsive to English learners, including programs for students with special gifts and talents.

- Ensure that students are placed in the least restrictive, most supportive environments possible for their identified learning needs.

Supporting Principle 3. *Design High-Quality Lessons for Language Development*

- Ensure that the curricula implemented in special education or gifted and talented program settings (both inclusion and stand-alone classroom settings) are linguistically and culturally responsive for dually identified English learners.

- Appreciate the role of the home language in the learning of English and help teachers connect instruction delivered in English at school with student's homes by using their home language. This may require having some dual language or home language–only materials available to send home for parents to work on with their child.

- Make sure that lessons delivered to English learners by special educators or gifted and talented program personnel follow the practices described in Chapter 3.

- Foster collaboration between English language teachers and special educators to ensure the delivery of high-quality instruction to English learners with disabilities. Likewise, foster collaboration between English language teachers and teachers working in gifted and talented programs to make instruction truly responsive to learners defined by both characteristics.

Supporting Principle 4. *Adapt Lesson Delivery as Needed*

- Provide teachers with funds from program budgets to purchase materials (instructional and supplemental) that can help meet the needs of diverse student populations.

- When evaluating special educators or teachers working in gifted and talented programs, give feedback about how well they are adapting their curriculum and instruction for identified English learners of diverse cultural backgrounds and varied proficiency levels.

- Offer staff development to your special educators and support staff or gifted and talented program personnel to help them understand and respond to important population shifts in your region.

Supporting Principle 5. *Monitor and Assess Student Language Development*

- Ensure that all personnel involved in administering and interpreting assessments conducted to determine students' eligibility for special education or gifted and talented programs are fully bilingual and bicultural. As needed, hire special education assessors who are bilingual, or, at a minimum, are trained to assess linguistically and culturally diverse students. If students are sufficiently proficient to allow some testing to be conducted in English, exercise caution in interpreting the results, fully accounting for the possible effects of language and culture on the student's performance.

- In cases where interpreters are used to administer eligibility assessments, maintain all best practice guidelines. (See "Best Practices in Working with Translators and Interpreters," on page 86.)

- Make sure that assessment measures used with English learners with identified disabilities take into account all primary characteristics of the learners—language, culture, and disability—in both their delivery and their interpretation.

- Ensure that English learners with disabilities are provided with all the accommodations to which they are entitled as English learners and as students with special learning needs (ETS, 2009; Young, 2008).

- When identifying students as gifted and talented, ensure that identification criteria are not biased against students who are in the process of learning English. Consider alternative assessments to identify English learners with special gifts and talents if program data show a pattern of under-enrollment of English learners in your programs.

Reading Specialists and Instructional Coaches

Reading specialists and instructional coaches are key players in advancing classroom practices to promote student achievement. They may work directly with students, model best practices in classrooms, or "push in" to co-teach in the classroom to deliver more responsive instruction to students. Chapter 3 provides extensive guidance concerning classroom practices that support effective instruction for English learners, and reading specialists and instructional coaches will certainly want to be well versed in all the teaching practices outlined there. In addition, if you are a reading special or instructional coach, you will want to take the actions recommended below to establish a shared culture of responsibility. These will help you ensure that all the teachers whom you support implement the 6 Principles and research-based teaching practices known to be effective with English learners.

Supporting Principle 1. *Know Your Learners*

Seeking Data Where Data Are Needed

As a result of a steep increase in English learner enrollment at a local middle school and high school, content teachers were offered targeted professional development. They received information about the languages and cultures of the students as well as about the district's English language proficiency assessment and how to interpret and use the scores. Special attention was given to ways of using the data to differentiate instruction in classrooms. However, as the workshop progressed, the teachers became frustrated when they learned that the district's electronic data management system did not include detailed language proficiency data. It listed only the students' overall proficiency level—not their abilities in listening, speaking, reading, and writing. Teachers were told to ask the ESL teachers in their schools for this information if they wanted it for guidance in differentiating instruction. The teachers were visibly upset: Given the importance of this information to their lesson planning, why wasn't it easily accessible in the online data management system?

- As you work with teachers, demonstrate your understanding of the differences between reading in a first language and reading in a second language by emphasizing meaning-based teaching approaches over rote- or discrete-skill teaching approaches. English learners need to learn small skills (such as phonics) within a meaningful, whole-text framework, so that the emphasis is on comprehension over rote decoding.

- If at all possible, help your school assess students' home language reading and writing abilities so that you know the status of the students' literacy in the home language as the students begin to learn to read and write in English. Locate literacy tests that are available in languages other than English for the major languages that make up your school community.

- As an instructional coach, make sure that all the teachers with whom you work know the proficiency levels of their students by language skill—specifically, their proficiency levels in listening, speaking, reading, and writing—not just an overall proficiency level. This information can help teachers know when to provide additional supports to students, based on their profile of skills. Some students may need extra support when listening to instruction delivered in English; others may need extra support when required to speak or write to show their understanding of concepts being taught. Help your school make this information readily available in its electronic data systems so that teachers can easily see the proficiency characteristics of their students for lesson planning and instructional delivery purposes.

- Make sure that the teachers with whom you work have easy access to information about their students' home language, cultural background, current stage of language proficiency (in listening, speaking, reading, and writing), as well as current literacy levels, so that that they can tailor instruction accordingly.

Supporting Principle 2. *Create Conditions for Language Learning*

- Take every opportunity to honor and affirm children's cultural and linguistic identities. Working with others, create schoolwide literacy events that highlight the multilingualism of your students and celebrate their backgrounds by inviting authors, poets, or journalists from their cultures or home language groups.

- Help identify materials written by authors who represent the cultural communities of your learners. Choose materials that have won respected awards or prizes (e.g., Pura Belpre Award, New Voices Award) and that represent the cultural worlds and life experiences of your learners. Share these materials with the teachers and families that you support.

- Take every opportunity to help teachers set up their classrooms in ways that are comfortable for learners from diverse cultural backgrounds. Consider grouping arrangements, the amount of talking permitted, use of the home language, expectations regarding students volunteering to respond, wait time, and so forth.

Supporting Principle 3. *Design High-Quality Lessons for Language Development*

Creating Lessons That Engage English Learners

An instructional coach spent the day observing content-area classes at one of the high schools in her district. As she sat in the back of a U.S. history class, she carefully watched the two English learners sitting by the window toward the back of the room. While the teacher was speaking to the class and pointing to terms on the board, the two students alternated between gazing out the window and sneaking glances at their cellphones. After a few minutes, a class discussion ensued, with the teacher calling on students who raised their hands. The two English learners kept their heads down, trying not to be noticed. They didn't have much to worry about since the teacher focused on other learners for the entire class period. When the instructional coach discussed her observations with the teacher after the lesson, the teacher said that she knew that the English learners didn't understand much of the lesson—she was just letting them absorb as much as they could.

As the preceding vignette illustrates, it's important for teachers to ensure that lessons are differentiated, relevant, and engaging for all students—not just to deliver lessons that are suitable for some but leave others to get what they can. To create and deliver high-quality lessons, teachers may need support. As a reading specialist or instructional coach, you are in a perfect position to aid teachers in fully understanding the characteristics of lessons that promote maximum language growth for English learners while imparting valuable content-area knowledge and skills. The following are actions that you can take to support teachers in designing high-quality lessons for language development:

- Guide teachers as they work to make their instruction linguistically and culturally responsive, and help them differentiate their instruction for English learners of all proficiency levels and cultural backgrounds. In particular, make sure that teachers understand the cultural dimensions present in classrooms and how they can shape instructional and social interactions to create positive learning conditions for learners of diverse backgrounds. Make sure that lessons delivered to English learners take into account their level of English proficiency and consider their background knowledge and cultural characteristics.

- Make sure that the teachers with whom you work know how to shape listening and speaking activities, as well as reading and writing activities for their students, depending on their current proficiency levels in English. See the guidelines detailed in Chapter 3.

- Make sure that the teachers whom you support understand the role that oral language and culturally determined background knowledge play in second language reading comprehension and writing performance. Show teachers how to frontload essential language and background information before engaging students in reading or writing activities.

- Share your knowledge of the language transfer process with other teachers—that knowing how to read and write in the home language positively affects reading and writing in English. Give examples of language transfer (e.g., finding the main idea, noticing English words that look like words in the home language) and help teachers learn how to enhance the transfer process during instruction. In particular, guide all teachers of reading to make connections with the skills and knowledge that second language readers bring to the act of reading or writing from their home language. Investigate the orthographies of the language groups that you serve to know what may or may not transfer to reading and writing in English; share this information with the teachers with whom you work.

- If you are a reading specialist, adopt research-based approaches to the teaching of reading and writing in a second language, and make sure that these approaches are in use in all instructional settings in which English learners participate.

- If you are an instructional coach, promote professional learning at your school related to the effective education of English learners, focusing on teaching strategies, materials, and programs. Adopt research-based teaching approaches specifically designed for English learners (e.g., sheltered instruction, bilingual and dual language instruction, technology-infused language instruction, and integrated skills development).

- Offer teachers well-selected materials to enhance learning for English learners and guide them in selecting or adapting instructional materials for students of varied proficiency levels. Help teachers understand the types of scaffolds to look for as they choose materials (e.g., captions, bolded words, clear illustrations and graphics that match the text, glossaries, audio versions of texts). Provide materials in the home language that can be used with English learners who are literate in their home languages to support content learning.

- In cases where you provide direct services to students, coordinate your work with the English language teachers; make sure that you are using the same research-based methods that they are using with the students. Where possible, maintain the themes that are in use in the classroom to deepen and enrich the language and literacy development of students.

Work collaboratively to develop high-quality lessons that simultaneously develop language and content.

- Help extend the high-quality language and literacy lessons delivered at school to student's homes and communities. Help the teachers whom you support send home dual language or home language books on the same theme to link family literacy activities to those going on at school.

- As an instructional coach, deliver in-class demonstration lessons to model the delivery of well-planned and high-quality lessons that embed language learning into content lesson sequences. Demonstrate how to promote academic language learning (Echevarría, Vogt, & Short, 2017; Stepanek & Raphael, 2010). Model lessons that promote language development and critical thinking across listening, speaking, reading, and writing for students of all proficiency levels.

Supporting Principle 4. *Adapt Lesson Delivery as Needed*

- If you are serving English learners with limited formal schooling and little or no literacy in their home language, ensure that the teachers you work with know how to begin literacy instruction at later ages than is typical.

- If you are an instructional coach, revisit the methods and materials that all teachers use to determine whether any changes are needed to respond well to new populations' language and literacy levels.

- For each ethnolinguistic group that you serve, consider important cultural dimensions that have an impact on the teaching-learning process, and ensure that the teachers with whom you work make their instruction culturally responsive and compatible so that all English learners can thrive.

- Find materials (fiction and informational texts) that reflect your school's linguistic and cultural groups and share them with all teachers so that the full student population is represented in the curriculum.

Supporting Principle 5. *Monitor and Assess Student Language Development*

Interpreting Statewide Assessment Data for Learners New to English

At the grade 4 team meeting, the math instructional coach and the ESL teacher carefully explained current testing policies requiring English learners to take the state mathematics test in English no matter when they arrived in the country, unless a home language test was available and a student was literate in that language. They also explained that scores obtained in English on the math test were not very reliable for new arrivals or English learners at the initial levels of English development.

As the grade 4 teachers reviewed the scores from the most recent statewide assessment, they were asked to put an asterisk next to the name of any English learner whom they knew either to be a new arrival when the test was taken or to have language proficiency scores at the two lowest levels. If the teachers were unsure of a student's proficiency level, the ESL teacher added that information. The math coach and the classroom teachers then reviewed all the names marked with asterisks and used their knowledge of the child in each case to determine which of the new arrivals or students at beginning proficiency levels would now receive additional support from the math coach. In cases where there was any doubt, the math coach scheduled the student for diagnostic testing with the aid of an interpreter to be sure that all students needing support received it. The ESL teacher and the math coach also determined which students would need to be in a team-teaching intervention group offered by the math coach with support from a bilingual assistant.

As noted earlier in the chapter, ESSA (2015) has made growth in English language proficiency a required indicator in every state's accountability system. Whether mandated by current federal legislation or not, all schools will want to make the education of their English learners a priority and demonstrate that they are improving students' English language proficiency, as well as their educational achievement. Ensuring that students are advancing in their learning of both language and content requires that the students receive the kind of instruction that can lead to their success. All school-based professionals will want to actively monitor student progress in language development and other content areas to make sure that English learners are progressing and that programs are working. But as a reading specialist or instructional coach, you will also want to interpret scores on statewide or district assessments fairly for English learners who only recently arrived or are at the lowest levels of English proficiency when tests are administered in English. The following are actions that you can take to aid in monitoring learners' progress and supporting their performance on assessments:

- Help teachers with whom you work design appropriate assessments that accommodate the language proficiency, literacy levels, cultural backgrounds, and prior testing experience of individual English learners (ETS, 2009).

- Make sure that all reading assessments are appropriate for students learning English as a new language and accurately assess the reading abilities of students in the process of learning English. Consider cultural bias, task bias, unknown vocabulary, and other language barriers.

- Help incorporate test-like tasks in ongoing classroom assessments to familiarize students with test formats and tasks that they will encounter when taking district and state assessments.

- Ensure that all assessments (e.g., running records, diagnostic reading tests, math tests, science tests) are appropriately administered to English learners and are interpreted with consideration of issues typically faced by students in the process of learning English (e.g., not being able to answer a question because of cultural bias or unknown vocabulary in the prompt).

- In cases where students are not making adequate progress, help teachers look for instructional or program weaknesses before attributing low performance to deficiencies in students. Work to correct program weaknesses so that students can succeed before attributing a test result to weakness or "failure" on the part of the students.

Supporting Principle 6. *Engage and Collaborate within a Community of Practice*

When Student Needs Change

As a result of an influx of recent refugees from war-torn countries, middle-level teachers in an urban school district in the Midwest noticed that among the district's newcomers were many students who had either not been to school consistently or had never been to school. These students were placed in middle school classes with other students who were beginners in English, but the ESL teacher, Ms. Manning, believed that their needs were not being adequately addressed. She didn't know how to give them the initial literacy instruction that they needed while also responding to the needs of the other beginners, who had strong or at least adequate literacy and educational backgrounds. She reached out to her reading specialist for assistance, but they were both unsure of the best way to initiate literacy instruction with older learners, and they didn't know what materials might be available for them. Luckily, they saw that their state TESOL affiliate was sponsoring a preconference session on exactly this topic. The ESL and reading teacher quickly signed up as a team, hoping they would get ideas about how to adapt their instruction for this special group of English learners and learn about methods and materials that they might use for initial literacy instruction.

It is not uncommon for districts to see changes in their English learner population from one year to the next. A district that has served a particular language group at one time may see the languages and cultures of their students change, sometimes rather dramatically. Or perhaps at one point the English learners in a district came with strong educational backgrounds, but now more refugees and asylum seekers with limited formal education are enrolling. Instruction that may have been working well for a certain population may need to be revisited as population changes occur. As a reading specialist or an instructional coach, you can work with classroom teachers as they adapt to these significant changes. The vignette provides an example of the benefits that come from these types of collaboration. The following are other actions that you can take to engage with the instructional personnel and help them deliver high-quality lessons to English learners:

- Bring all instructional personnel together in making decisions about students; respect the knowledge and skills of each person and use their expertise in forming instructional plans for English learners.

- Collaborate with all instructional personnel delivering instruction in order to align your work philosophically and strategically. More specifically, ensure that all instructional personnel use research-based approaches designed for English learners, together with materials known to be effective with students in the process of learning English.

- Continue your own personal, professional, and role-specific growth to enhance service delivery to English learners. There is always more to learn and many ways to advance professionally for the benefit of students.

- Help form school-based study groups to promote growth for teams of professionals in the use of best practices for English learners.

Librarians and Media Specialists

School librarians and media specialists serve their schools in an essential capacity. They build and maintain rich instructional collections of print and multimedia resources that serve teachers, students, and families. Librarians and media specialists also promote literacy and content learning through their interactions with students. If you are a school librarian or media specialist, you are in a perfect position to support teachers as they seek culturally and linguistically responsive materials for their students. You can contribute immeasurably to the learning that goes on in school and at home by locating and adding to your collections the needed resources for teachers, students, and parents. In these ways, you play an important role in supporting the full implementation of the 6 Principles. Some key actions are described below.

Supporting Principle 1. *Know Your Learners*

Developing Literacy Skills in Parents and Children

Taking a page from the local library's playbook, Beaumont Elementary School's librarian decided to offer a bilingual story time once a month. She scheduled this event for ten minutes after the school day ended, so that parents who came to pick up their children could bring them to the library for a snack and a story. Younger siblings were welcome. The librarian, who was studying Spanish as a second language herself, read two books aloud each month—one fiction and one nonfiction, on related topics. Sometimes a parent helped her with the pronunciation of unfamiliar words! She modeled how parents could read such books at home, doing a picture walk before reading, asking high-level questions about the text while reading, and making connections to other stories that they knew. At the end of the reading time, parents could use their children's school ID cards to check out books to bring home.

- Educate yourself about the levels of proficiency through which English learners progress so that you can identify materials that support learners at each level.

- Ensure that the resource collection that you manage is responsive to English learners of all proficiency levels and cultural backgrounds and connects with their life experiences.

- Affirm the identities of your English learners by mounting displays that show the richness of students' cultural worlds (e.g., exhibits of books from students' countries of origin; collections of materials about artists, authors, musicians, scientists, or historical figures from students' cultural and geographic backgrounds).

- Create online and print collections in the home languages of your students and families so that home language materials are available to support learning. Allow students to use these resources at school or at home, and encourage younger learners to bring texts or online resources home to involve their parents in literacy activities and content learning. These collections should include fiction and nonfiction texts, hi-lo readers, magazines, periodicals, audiobooks, maps, reference materials, and multimedia.

- Make sure that the library has bilingual dictionaries in the major home languages.

Supporting Principle 3. *Design High-Quality Lessons for Language Development*

- Create collections of resources, including multimedia resources, both in English and in the home languages of the students, to support teachers in their work with English learners of all proficiency and literacy levels.

- Locate parallel materials in the students' home languages for the main curriculum units at each grade level, and make that material available to classroom teachers and reading and learning specialists.

- Bookmark key websites on the library's computers for translations, home language readings, home language newspapers, and student-oriented research.

- Welcome parents to the school library, and hold outreach events so that parents know the resources and services that you can provide. Encourage parents to take out books in the home language and English to read at home with their children. Make sure that parents know the importance of continuing to develop the home language and how doing so contributes children's English learning and academic success.

Supporting Principle 6. *Engage and Collaborate within a Community of Practice*

- Work with classroom teachers and language specialists to design lessons that orient English learners to the school library, and teach them how to use it effectively, including how to access helpful materials online.

- Reach out to public librarians, and assist English learners and their families in becoming members of their public libraries. Help them understand how to use their local libraries, including locating collections in their home language and using services that may be offered to adults (such as ESL, citizenship, or technology classes) or to children (such as book clubs and story hour). Make sure that they feel safe in using public libraries and know that they cannot be asked for their legal status as a condition for library membership.

Guidance Counselors, Social Workers, and School Psychologists

School guidance counselors, social workers, and school psychologists bring special expertise to the team of practitioners working to meet the needs of English learners and their families. If you are a guidance counselor, social worker, or school psychologist, most likely you have a rich background and strong understanding of cultural diversity and all the implications for providing responsive services to students and families. However, you may not be as well versed in second language development or how to deliver educational and counseling services to learners who are still in the process of learning English. As you receive new ethnolinguistic groups of students in your district or school, you may need to learn about the home languages and cultures of students and families that you are new to serving, just as much as the classroom personnel whom you work to support. This section outlines actions that you can take to help your district or school as it works to implement the 6 Principles in its efforts to provide a high-quality education for English learners.

Making Multilingualism the Norm

Mr. Lakin, a bilingual social studies teacher, and Ms. Leininger, an ESL teacher, noticed that the parents of their English learners were not participating at open houses or other school functions at their suburban high school. They decided to take action to see whether they could change the situation. They contacted the bilingual guidance counselor to develop a plan of action. First, they made signs for every classroom in the school, listing the name of the teacher and the languages that the teacher spoke. Next, they created a student club called Language Ambassadors. To participate in the club, students had to speak English and another language of the school community well. Before each school event, the Language Ambassadors worked under the guidance of the guidance counselor to call homes and personally invite parents, explaining the purpose of the function, mentioning that they would be there to greet them, and answering any questions that parents had about the event. The night of the first school event, the Language Ambassadors wore signs with their names and the languages that they spoke, and they greeted parents at the door. Then each Language Ambassador met with parents who spoke a given language in a separate orientation room to give an overview of the evening's event. The two teachers were astonished. In less than six months, and with only these two strategies in place, they went from a school with less than 10 percent of language minority parent participating on average to one where 70 percent of their students' parents came to school events designed for families.

Supporting Principle 1. *Know Your Learners*

- Work with family liaisons to share information with all instructional personnel about the cultures of your English learners and their families and the communities in which they live. In particular, ensure that all personnel serving English learners are familiar with the most important cultural norms that make home-school interactions successful and comfortable. Inform teachers of any sensitive or taboo topics and how to handle these in the classroom.

- Make sure that all school personnel know the language or languages in which families would like to receive information from the school, and whether they prefer to receive information orally or in writing. Find out their preferred communication mode—printed material, phone, text message, or email, and share this information with key personnel. Try to determine the literacy levels of parents by inquiring about the levels of education they were able to complete, so you can be sure that you are communicating effectively with your families.

- Ensure that all personnel working with English learners have all the information that is available about their students and their families, particularly about their educational histories and prior educational programming, as well as any socioemotional needs of learners.

- Learn about parents' expectations for their child's schooling and the culturally determined roles that parents typically play in their child's education. Share this information so that all school personnel understand the many traditional roles that parents play in the education of their children from a cross-cultural perspective.

- Assist all school personnel in appreciating and responding to the academic, career, personal, and social needs of English learners. As you work with students, ensure that students receive culturally responsive personal and social support to facilitate their academic success and personal growth. Actively collaborate with ESL and bilingual teachers to make sure that the instructional needs of English learners are being fully met.

- Be sensitive to and ensure that all school personnel are aware of issues relating to the possible undocumented status of students and/or family members. Consult organizations such as the ACLU and the Southern Poverty Law Center (which publishes the magazine *Teaching Tolerance*) to be clear about the rights of undocumented students and families. Learn about ways of supporting undocumented students enrolled in your school (including those who were eligible for Deferred Action for Childhood Arrivals [DACA]); useful approaches are outlined by the Harvard Graduate School of Education. (See "Resources to Support Undocumented Families and DACA Students" below.) Also be aware that the threat of deportation (either for themselves or a family member) may create great stress for some learners and have an impact on their performance and behavior in school.

Resources to Support Undocumented Families and DACA Youth

ACLU of Arizona (www.acluaz.org/en/publications/fact-sheet-undocumented-students-families -school)

Harvard Graduate School of Education (www.gse.harvard.edu/news/uk/17/02/supporting -undocumented-students).

National Immigration Law Center (www.nilc.org)

Teaching Tolerance (www.tolerance.org/magazine/spring-2017/immigrant-and-refugee-children -a-guide-for-educators-and-school-support-staff)

- Depending on your state, some undocumented high schoolers may not eligible for in-state tuition if they are accepted at a state university. None will be able to receive federal financial aid. Keep these limitations in mind when planning postsecondary options with them.

- Ensure that English learners have access to both special education and gifted and talented services, as appropriate, and that parents understand these programs. Limited language proficiency in English should not be a barrier to their access to these services (Seddon, 2015; USED & USDOJ, 2015).

Supporting Principle 2. *Create Conditions for Language Learning*

- Take care to account fully for the previous educational experiences of students, both to make appropriate grade placements and to award high school credits fairly.

- Ensure that English learners are placed into appropriate programs on the basis of their educational characteristics and the expressed goals of their families (e.g., placement in a bilingual, ESL, or dual language program; referrals to gifted and talented programs).

- Share intake information with all teachers who serve English learners so that they have as much information about their students as possible. Be sure that they know the basics about their students: their home language; educational background; cultural background; current English proficiency levels in listening, speaking, reading, and writing; a current English reading score determined by using developmental systems such as Fountas and Pinnell, Developmental Reading Assessment (DRA), or Lexile; and, if possible, their reading level in the home language.

Supporting Principle 3. *Design High-Quality Lessons for Language Development*

- Share information with teachers about the socioemotional status of English learners so that they can make lessons responsive to the personal and social needs of students.

- Share information with teachers about community resources that can enrich the lessons that they plan—local cultural or art museums, community centers, and individuals who possess special talents and skills and live in the local cultural communities of the school.

Supporting Principle 5. *Monitor and Assess Student Language Development*

- Make sure that parental reporting systems are well designed, accessible, and easy to interpret so that language minority parents can easily understand how their children are doing. Make sure that they are written in the parents' preferred language or mode of communication.

- Educate parents about your state's language proficiency measures; make sure that they understand the expected amount of growth that students should attain from one year to the next, depending on their starting level.

- Inform parents about the meaning and purpose of district and state assessments.

- If you are involved in special education assessments or the identification of students with special gifts and talents, you may want to review relevant resources and recommendations in the section "Special Education Directors and Gifted and Talented Program Directors" earlier in this chapter.

Supporting Principle 6. *Engage and Collaborate within a Community of Practice*

- Educate parents and students about the local school system; attendance, promotion and graduation requirements; grade-level learning expectations; grading practices; and postsecondary options for high school students.

- Lead outreach efforts to the school's language and cultural communities; share resources and connections with all school personnel. Serve as a liaison to home and community and coordinate with family liaisons that work in your school or district's English learner programs.

- Build your knowledge of local linguistic and cultural resources that the school can tap as needed. Partner with community services that may help families with social, health, lodging, and employment concerns. Identify community resources that may be helpful for teachers to know about in order to give their students outside school support as they adjust to their school and community.

- Ensure that students and parents feel safe and secure and that confidentiality is maintained. Ensure that all families feel respected and included in decisions affecting their children's educational futures.

A Look Back and a Final Observation

Chapter 5 examines the roles of a range of school-based professionals whose work complements that of classroom-based staff in supporting the education of English learners. For each group of practitioners, the chapter has outlined key actions and offered helpful resources to aid in the full implementation of the 6 Principles for exemplary teaching of English learners. In making these recommendations, the chapter has highlighted the following ideas, based on research and best practice:

- Successful programs depend on establishing a strong culture of shared responsibility for English learners and their families.

- English learners and their families bring linguistic and cultural resources to the school and classroom. These assets should be welcomed, promoted, and fully used to strengthen teaching and learning. This cannot be accomplished unless we take time to investigate the linguistic and cultural resources possessed by our English learners and their families.

- Equity and access can be achieved only if all professionals work together to ensure that English learners receive high-quality programs and services designed to support their educational success in a positive, welcoming school climate.

- All personnel can aid in the delivery of high-quality lessons for language and content development, adapting instruction as needed for key learner characteristics. They can also assist in monitoring and assessing students' language development and academic achievement in ways that are culturally and linguistically appropriate, valid, and fair.

- School and district administrators, reading specialists and instructional coaches, librarians and media specialists, guidance counselors, social workers, and school psychologists can ensure the success of English learners when they consider their educational needs carefully and act on them.

A final observation: This chapter focuses on school-based professionals as key educators who are most able to implement the 6 Principles, but they are not alone. Many other professionals are involved in the education of English learners, including school board members, state policy-makers, and curriculum and test developers, who, despite their distance from the classroom, affect the education of English learners. Test developers and curriculum writers have a direct impact on students; they can either support or frustrate the success of English learners by the way in which their products are designed and implemented or interpreted. School board members and other policymakers affect the education of English learners by the educational policies that they adopt, the curricula and assessments that they approve, and the human and material resources that they make available to schools.

State education departments and teacher educators are also critical players in the delivery of programs to English learners. The former create the conditions necessary for local schools to succeed through the funding that they allocate and the regulations that they issue, and the latter prepare future personnel who will work in the schools. Indeed, teacher education institutions and schools are partners in the preparation of future teachers of English learners, and, as such, they will find that this volume contains valuable information for them as they work together to prepare teachers who will serve English learners across their professional careers.

Indeed, all the professionals named here can benefit by reviewing *The 6 Principles for Exemplary Teaching of English Learners* so that they can honor the principles as they fulfill their important roles.

Additional resources pertaining to this chapter, are available in Appendix C, "Resources for Key Personnel Who Share Responsibility for the Education of English Learners" and www.the6principles.org/K-12.

APPENDIXES
GLOSSARY
REFERENCES
AND FURTHER READING

Overview of the Most Common Programs for English Learners in the United States

	ESL/ELD/Sheltered Programs			Newcomer Programs	Bilingual Programs		
	ESL/ELD	Content-based ESL	Sheltered		Transitional Bilingual	Dual language/Two-way Immersion	Bilingual content areas
Class Types Note: Federal law requires educational services for English learners, but the type of program may be set by state or local policy.	May be pull-out, push-in, or self-contained	May be pull-out, push-in, or self-contained Also known as Designated ELD	Sheltered instruction in content areas Self-contained Also known as Integrated ELD or SDAIE (Specially-designed academic instruction in English)	Content-based ESL, basic literacy, some sheltered instruction or native language content instruction Self-contained	Transitional Bilingual: ESL + all other content areas in native language of students Self-contained May be early exit or late exit, depending on language goals	Dual language/Two-way Immersion: All content areas in one of the two languages (sheltered instruction in either language when non-native speakers are present) Self-contained	Bilingual content areas At secondary level, some courses are offered in the native language of some students Self-contained
Language Goals	English proficiency, some focus on academic English	Academic English proficiency	Academic English proficiency	English development (typically to advanced beginner level); some programs have native language development	Transition to all-English instruction; limited native language development for early exit, more native language development for late exit	Bilingualism (in target language and English) Usually goals for target and American culture	Limited native language development (except for native language arts classes)
Academic Content Goals	Same as district/program goals for all students	Same as district/program goals for all students	Same as district/program goals for all students	Varied (depends on length of program and hours/day)	Same as district/program goals for all students	Same as district/program goals for all students	Same as district/program goals for all students

(continued)

Overview of the Most Common Programs for English Learners in the United States						
	ESL/ELD/Sheltered Programs			Newcomer Programs	Bilingual Programs		
Language of Instruction	English, some native language for clarification or support	English, some native language for clarification or support	English, some native language for clarification or support	English and/or native language for some content areas or for clarification and support	Native language for content areas + English	Target language and English for content areas; may begin with 90% of day in native language and taper to 50%, or may be at 50% for each language throughout	Native language
Student Characteristics	Limited or no English / Variety of language/cultural backgrounds	Limited or no English / Variety of language/cultural backgrounds	Limited or no English / Variety of language/cultural backgrounds / Some programs mix native and non-native English speakers in certain courses	Limited or no English / Typically low-level literacy in native language / Recent arrival / May have had limited or interrupted schooling / Variety of language/cultural backgrounds	Limited or no English / All students have same native language / May have a variety of cultural backgrounds	Language-majority (usually English) and language-minority students (usually speakers of the target language, often limited in English); some dual language programs have only students with same native language / Variety of cultural backgrounds	Limited or no English / All students have same native language / May have a variety of cultural backgrounds
Grades Served	All grades (during transition to general education)	All grades (during transition to general education)	All grades (during transition to general education)	2–12; most prevalent at secondary school levels	Primary and elementary grades, rare at secondary school levels	K–5, K–8, a few K–12	Mostly at high school, some at middle school

(continued)

Overview of the Most Common Programs for English Learners in the United States

	ESL/ELD/Sheltered Programs			Newcomer Programs	Bilingual Programs		
Length of Student Participation	Varied: Typically 1–5 years or as needed	Varied: Typically 1–5 years or as needed	Varied: 1–3 years or as needed	Usually 1–3 semesters	Usually 1–2 years for early exit; 3–5 years for late exit	Usually 5–6 years; some continue 8 or 12 years (+ K)	Varied: 1–2 years or as needed
Teachers Note: Credentials vary by state	ESL/ELD certified teachers	ESL/ELD certified teachers	Usually grade-level classroom and content teachers who are ESL-endorsed and/or have training in sheltered instruction May be co-taught	ESL/ELD/ Bilingual teachers; sometimes grade-level classroom and content teachers who are ESL-endorsed and/or have training in sheltered instruction	Bilingual teachers	Bilingual teachers; grade-level classroom and content teachers with bilingual proficiency and training in sheltered instruction May be co-taught	Bilingual teachers with content area certification

Sources:

California Department of Education. (2010). *Improving education for English learners: Research-based approaches.* Sacramento, CA: CDE Press.

Echevarria, J., Vogt, ME., & Short, D. (2017). *Making content comprehensible for English learners: The SIOP Model* (5th ed.). Boston, MA: Pearson.

Genesee, F. (Ed.). (1999). *Program alternatives for linguistically diverse students.* Educational Practice Report No. 1. Santa Cruz, CA, & Washington, DC: Center for Research on Education, Diversity, & Excellence.

Howard, E., & Sugarman, J. (2007). *Realizing the vision of two-way immersion: Fostering effective programs and classrooms.* Washington, DC: Center for Applied Linguistics.

Short, D., & Boyson, B. (2012). *Helping newcomer students succeed in secondary schools and beyond.* Washington, DC: Center for Applied Linguistics.

U.S. Department of Education, Office for Civil Rights, & U.S. Department of Justice, Civil Rights Division. (2015). *Dear colleague letter: English learner students and limited English proficient parents.* Washington, DC: Author. Retrieved from www2.ed.gov/about/offices/list/ocr/letters/colleague-el-201501.pdf

Appendix B
Self-Assessment: The 6 Principles Checklist for Teachers

Do you know your learners? (Principle 1)

___ **You gain information about your learners.**

For example, you

- ___ conduct intake protocols and a needs assessment
- ___ collect and/or review linguistic and educational background information from the district home language survey
- ___ organize and share information with other teachers.

___ **You embrace and leverage the resources your learners bring to the classroom to enhance learning.**

For example, you

- ___ collect resources about your students' cultures and languages
- ___ gather information from parents and guardians about your students' personal and cultural experiences and language practices in the home
- ___ engage students in activities that allow them to share their personal lives, culture, and experiences with the class
- ___ act as a cultural mediator for students and their families with others in the school system.

Do you create conditions for language learning? (Principle 2)

___ **You promote a positive and organized classroom with attention to reducing student anxiety and developing trust.**

For example, you

- ___ create a welcoming environment for the students
- ___ design appropriate work spaces
- ___ organize the physical environment for individual and group work and for student-student communication
- ___ identify mentors for new students
- ___ use clear, patterned, and routine language to communicate with new learners
- ___ invite and support use of student home languages and cultures in lessons.

___ **You demonstrate expectations of success for all your learners.**

For example, you

- ___ believe all students will learn academic English and content to a high level
- ___ praise effort and persistence
- ___ use a variety of instructional approaches for diverse learners
- ___ teach learners strategies to participate in instructional conversations.

___ **You plan instruction to enhance and support student motivation for language learning.**

For example, you

- ___ prompt students to connect their learning to their own lives
- ___ build a repertoire of learning tasks that students enjoy
- ___ motivate students and structure behavior with projects
- ___ expect student ownership and support students in engagement with learning.

Do you **design high-quality lessons for language development? (Principle 3)**

___ **You prepare lessons with clear outcomes and convey them to your students.**

For example, you

___ determine content and language objectives for your lessons

___ communicate learning objectives to students.

___ **You provide and enhance input through varied approaches, techniques, and modalities.**

For example, you

___ use comprehensible input to convey information to students

___ adjust your language to enhance input to students

___ use multiple sources of input

___ communicate clear instructions for lesson tasks.

___ **You engage learners in the use and practice of authentic language.**

For example, you

___ elicit output from students

___ create opportunities for learners to be active participants

___ use techniques to promote active language practice throughout the lesson

___ integrate language learning into content lessons and content into language lessons

___ encourage language learning beyond the classroom.

___ **You design lessons so students engage with relevant and meaningful content.**

For example, you

___ plan culturally relevant and interesting tasks

___ select materials that reflect student interests.

___ **You plan differentiated instruction according to your learners' English language proficiency levels, needs, and goals.**

For example, you

___ build scaffolding into lessons for different purposes

___ employ grouping patterns designed to promote peer support, engagement, and comprehensibility

___ provide supplemental materials

___ plan for appropriate challenge depending on learner language proficiency levels.

___ **You promote use of learning strategies and critical thinking among your students.**

For example, you

___ teach a variety of learning strategies for specific purposes

___ design tasks for students to practice using critical thinking and learning strategies.

___ **You promote self-regulated learning among your students.**

For example, you

___ facilitate students' setting of meaningful goals and monitoring of their progress

___ provide self-assessment tools that allow students to evaluate their strengths and weaknesses

___ help students develop effective study habits.

Do you **adapt lesson delivery as needed? (Principle 4)**

___ **You check student comprehension frequently and adjust instruction according to learner responses.**

For example, you

___ use teaching practices that ensure better auditory comprehension

___ check comprehension with group response techniques.

___ **You adjust your talk, the task, or the materials according to learner responses.**

For example, you

___ adjust your oral language input as needed to advance comprehension and scaffold academic language learning

___ switch to other forms of input as needed

___ adapt tasks and/or materials to learner proficiency levels

___ scaffold extensively to provide equitable access to content for all learners.

Do you **monitor and assess student language development? (Principle 5)**

___ **You monitor your students' errors.**

For example, you

___ note errors to provide appropriate feedback to students

___ reteach when errors indicate students misunderstood or learned the material incorrectly.

___ **You provide ongoing effective feedback strategically.**

For example, you

___ use specific feedback

___ deliver feedback in a timely manner

___ deliver feedback according to the age and proficiency level of your learners

___ use a variety of types of oral corrective feedback

___ use written feedback when appropriate.

___ **You design varied and valid assessments and supports to assess your students' learning.**

For example, you

___ use classroom-based assessment to inform teaching and improve learning

___ use testing procedures based on principles of assessment

___ rely on a variety of assessment types.

Do you **engage and collaborate within a community of practice? (Principle 6)**

___ **You are fully engaged in your profession.**

For example, you

___ engage in reflective practice

___ participate in continuous learning and ongoing professional development.

___ **You collaborate with other teachers to co-plan and co-teach.**

For example, you

___ meet with colleagues regularly to co-plan for future learning

___ develop and strengthen relationships with school colleagues that facilitate co-teaching

___ develop leadership skills to become a resource in your school.

Appendix C
Resources for Key Personnel Who Share Responsibility for the Education of English Learners

Resources for School Leaders

A Guide for Engaging ELL Families: Twenty Strategies for School Leaders
Breiseth, L. (2011). With K. Robertson and S. Lafond. Arlington, VA: Colorín Colorado (WETA Public Broadcasting).

Divided into six sections, this helpful guide offers twenty concrete ways of establishing strong relationships with English learners' families. It covers connecting with families, communicating important information, parent participation, parents as leaders, community partnerships, and creating a plan. Recommended resources are also listed, and helpful examples are provided throughout the guide. For the guide and related video clips, go to http://www.colorincolorado.org/guide/guide-engaging-ell -families-twenty-strategies-school-leaders

What School Leaders Need to Know about English Learners
Dormer, J. (2016). Alexandria, VA: TESOL Press. Co-published with the National Association of Secondary School Principals.

This volume, designed for administrators, is organized according to a set of essential questions that frame effective education for English learners. It introduces research-based strategies and best practices and helps illustrate how to design, develop, and lead English language programs that work. It includes a professional development guide and "Grab and Go" online resources designed for busy administrators to share with their teachers and staff.

English Language Learners at School: A Guide for Administrators (2nd ed.)
Hamayan, E., & Freeman Field, R. (Eds.) (2012). Philadelphia, PA: Caslon.

Experts answer over eighty questions from teachers and administrators. Specialists in the field provide clear, concise, and practical responses that teachers, administrators, and team members can readily apply to their schools and districts. The focus of the volume is on shared leadership and responsibility, action planning, professional development, and decision-making.

Effective Schooling for English Language Learners:
What Elementary School Principals Should Know and Do
Smiley, P., & Salsberry, T. (2007). Larchmont, NY: Eye on Education.

After providing a review of the need for change in schools, this volume offers chapters on second language acquisition and instructional strategies, home language instruction and support, student assessment, supportive schoolwide climate and organizational structures, and building the context for sustainable change. Each chapter focuses on what principals should know and do. The volume provides many self-assessment checklists, charts, rubrics, model forms, and questionnaires, as well as questions for reflection for each of the six chapters.

Resources for Special Education Directors or Gifted and Talented Program Directors

Implementing RTI with English Learners
Fisher, D., Frey, N., & Rothenberg, C. (2010). Bloomington, IN: Solution Tree.

Presents an approach designed to ensure that English learners have access to the core curriculum and achieve at high levels. The authors provide a framework for instruction and distinguish between high-quality instruction for English learners and high-quality instruction for all learners. In the core of the book, they describe Tier 1 and 2 assessments and supplemental interventions that build language and content knowledge, as well as intensive Tier 3 interventions. They describe how to distinguish between language difference and learning disability. The book is designed to assist in reviewing a school's or district's RtI policies. A downloadable study guide is available at www.solution-tree.com

Special Education Considerations for English Language Learners:
Delivering a Continuum of Services (2nd ed.)
Hamayan, E., Marler, B., Sanchez-Lopez, C., & Damico, J. (2013). Philadelphia, PA: Caslon.

Divided into twelve chapters, this resource book takes readers through the entire process of designing a continuum of services for English learners. The authors present a framework that systematically explores seven integral factors in order to design responsive services and programs for ELs. The authors recommend a collaborative service delivery model that takes advantage of the professional knowledge and skills of English language specialists as well as special education and other school-based service providers. Chapter 4 describes the RtI process for ELs, and chapters 5–11 systematically discuss the seven integral factors to consider when designing programs for English learners. This is an excellent book for joint professional development in which teams engage in study circles to plan a responsive RtI process for ELs.

Developing a Culturally and Linguistically Responsive Approach to Response to
Instruction & Intervention (RtI²) for English Language Learners
WIDA Consortium. (2013). Madison, WI: Board of Regents of the University of Wisconsin System, WIDA Consortium.

This resource explains seven integral factors to consider when planning responsive instruction and intervention for English learners experiencing learning difficulties. It also discusses what Tier 1, 2, and 3 instruction should look like for English learners. WIDA resources to screen, assess, and monitor progress in language development are identified, and useful checklists, sample protocols, and other resources for RtI teams are included. Available at: https://www.wida.us/get.aspx?id=601

Identifying Gifted and Talented English Language Learners, Grades K–12.
Iowa Department of Education & Connie Belin and Jacqueline N. Blank International Center for Gifted Education and Talent Development. (2008). Des Moines, IA: Iowa Department of Education.

This sixty-five-page manual is designed to assist districts in identifying gifted and talented English language learners. It provides recommended practices for identifying students along with strategies for advocating for students once they are identified, so that they have equitable access to the programs and services they need. A companion CD-ROM provides helpful tools and resources, such as student interview protocols and descriptions of successful programs. Available at https://www.educateiowa.gov/sites/files/ed/documents/IdentifyGiftedTalentedELL.pdf

Resources for Reading Specialists and Instructional Coaches

Literacy Instruction for ELLs
http://www.colorincolorado.org/literacy-instruction-ells

This section of the popular Colorín Colorado website for teachers of English learners provides information on early literacy instruction, reading instruction in grades 1–3 and 4–12, reading comprehension, close reading, nonfiction reading, reading engagement, and writing instruction for English learners. It includes articles and videos, research and reports, and blog posts that are very useful to reading specialists working with teachers of English learners. For books for teachers to use for professional study circles, see http://www.colorincolorado.org/booklist/reading-instruction-ells

The Coaching and Self-Reflection Tool for Competency in Teaching English Learners
Aligned to the Connecticut Common Core of Teaching Rubric for Effective Teaching 2016
Connecticut State Department of Education. (2017). Hartford, CT: Author.

Organized by phases of instruction (planning, implementing, and assessing instruction), this tool aids instructional coaches and the teachers that they work with in evaluating how well they are teaching English learners and identifying areas for improvement. Throughout, it provides sample coaching and reflection questions to guide instructional conversations among teachers and their coaches. A rich and useful tool for instructional coaches, this resource is available at http://www.sde.ct.gov/sde/lib/sde/pdf/publications/el/coaching_tool_for_competency_in_teaching_english_learners.pdf

Resources for School Librarians and Media Specialists

10 Ways to Support ELLs in the School Library
Jules, J. (n.d.). Retrieved from http://www.colorincolorado.org/article/10-ways-support-ells-school-library

This article outlines concrete actions that librarians can take to make their school library more welcoming for and supportive of English learners. A companion video is presented at the end of the article. On the Colorín Colorado website, see also "School Libraries & ELLs" at http://www.colorincolorado.org/school-support/school-libraries-ells

Resources for School Guidance Counselors, Social Workers, or School Psychologists

Newcomer Toolkit
U.S. Department of Education. (2016). Washington, DC: Author.

After defining the newcomer population, this 159-page resource discusses how to provide a safe and thriving school environment, high-quality instruction, and ways to respond to newcomers' social and emotional needs. A chapter on establishing partnerships with families is rich with family engagement tactics. Available at https://www2.ed.gov/about/offices/list/oela/newcomers-toolkit/ncomertoolkit.pdf

Partnering with Parents and Families to Support Immigrant and Refugee Children at School
Kugler, E. G. (2009). Washington, DC: Center for Health and Health Care in Schools, School of Public Health and Health Services, George Washington University.

Discusses ways to work with the families of immigrant and refugee students both to empower parents and to ensure students' access to supportive mental health-care services. The author describes model programs and shares ways of offering school-based mental health services. She also discusses ways of increasing the cultural competence of service providers. Available at www.lacgc.org/pdf/Partnering SupportImmigrantChildren.pdf

Online Resources for All Educators

www.sealofbiliteracy.org

Teachers of English learners can advocate for the Seal of Biliteracy to be affixed on the diploma of students who have reached proficiency in two or more languages. This website notes which states have adopted it and which are considering it. It explains why it is important and the steps that educators can follow to promote it.

https://cbitsprogram.org/

Teachers of English learners who know or suspect that some of their students have experienced trauma, either before or during their journeys to the United States, can explore Cognitive Behavioral Intervention in Schools (CBITS) as a possible support for these students.

http://www.colorincolorado.org/special-education-ell/resources

The Colorín Colorado website has links to articles, as well as resources developed by several states, to help educators follow appropriate procedures for identifying English learners with disabilities.

http://classroom.synonym.com/plan-family-literacy-night-school-4499292.html and http://www.adlit.org/article/42781/

Teachers of English learners will find many ideas for helping to welcome families of English learners into our school communities.

http://www.brycs.org/documents/upload/Interpretation-Translation-FAQ.pdf

Bridging Refugee Youth & Children's Services (BRYCS) has developed *Refugee Children in U.S. Schools: A Toolkit for Teachers and School Personnel* (Tool #5), which outlines federal requirements for providing interpretation/translation in schools. The document includes links to legislation and other helpful resources.

Glossary

Academic language: A register of the English language; the formal variety of language used for academic purposes (e.g., in academic conversations, lectures, and textbooks) and connected with literacy and academic achievement. Includes reading, writing, listening, and speaking skills used to acquire new knowledge and accomplish academic tasks. In the United States, sometimes known as *academic English*.

Accommodation: In the context of testing, a change in an assessment itself or the way in which it is administered, intended to make the test results more accurate by creating conditions that allow a test taker to demonstrate his or her knowledge or skills. Examples include allowing extended time and permitting the use of a bilingual glossary.

Authentic language: Language that has not been modified or simplified. Typically refers to language that is written for a native-speaking or proficient audience and created by a native speaker to convey a message.

Benchmark assessment: A short assessment administered at regular intervals to give teachers feedback on how well students are meeting the academic standards that have been set; a tool to measure student growth and tailor curriculum or design an intervention to meet individual learning needs. Sometimes known as *formative assessment*.

Bilingual education: A school program using two languages, typically the native language of some students and a target language. The amount of time and the subject(s) in each language depend on the type of bilingual program, its specific objectives, and students' level of language proficiency. (See Appendix A.)

Collocations: Words or terms that occur together in a language more frequently than chance would predict and that are used as fixed expressions (e.g., *fast food*, *take a break*, *go online*).

Common Core State Standards (CCSS): A set of standards published in 2010 by the National Governors Association Center for Best Practices and the Council of Chief State School Officers, intended to bring coherence to what is taught in grades K–12 in English language arts and literacy in history/social studies, science, and technical subjects and for mathematics in the United States. Adopted by most states in the United States, plus the District of Columbia and some U.S. territories.

Community of practice: A group of people who engage in a process of collective learning as they practice their profession. Each group member brings his or her own skill set, and the group actively shares knowledge, resources, experiences, and orientations to their work, while strengthening their relationships with one another, to enhance their collaborative efforts. Coined by Lave and Wegner (1991).

Comprehensible input: Oral or written input (e.g., new information) to the learner, structured or presented in such a way as to help him or her negotiate the meaning of the communication (e.g., through visuals, gestures, annotations). Over time, the input may increase in complexity of the language structures used or the amount of information shared.

Content-based ESL: An approach to instruction in which content topics are used as the vehicle for learning a new language—in this case, English. Teachers use a variety of techniques to help students develop language, content knowledge, and study skills. Instruction may be delivered through thematic units and tied to the subject-area instruction that English learners receive in grade-level and content area classrooms. (See Appendix A.)

Cultural diversity: The variety of cultures that students have in a classroom or school. Culture includes the customs, lifestyle, traditions, attitudes, norms of behavior, and artifacts of a given people. Culturally diverse students may have different races, ethnicities, languages, and socioeconomic status. A goal in the classroom is to respect and honor the diverse cultures and build on different ways of knowing or interpreting the world.

Culturally responsive instruction: An approach to classroom instruction that respects and builds on the different cultural characteristics of all students and ensures that academic discussions are open to different cultural views and perspectives. Student ways of knowing are elicited, pedagogical materials are multicultural, and values are shared and affirmed. Also known as *culturally responsive teaching* or *culturally relevant teaching*.

Discourse: A sequence of utterances—spoken or written sentences—that form a larger unit in a specific social context. For example, a dinner conversation, an academic lecture, a weather report, a kindergarten show-and-tell.

Dual language program: A type of bilingual education in which the goal is bilingualism and students study literacy and content in two languages—the students' home language and the target language (e.g., Spanish and English). The amount of time and subject(s) in each language may vary by design. Some dual language programs have native speakers of English and native speakers of the target language (e.g., Spanish); others have speakers that come from the same language background. Sheltered instruction is needed in classes when non-native speakers are present and learning through a language in which they are not proficient. A dual language teacher may teach through both languages or may be paired with another teacher who teaches through one of the languages. (See Appendix A.)

Dynamic bilingualism: The ability to use more than one language flexibly and strategically, depending on the audience, conversational partners, or the situation.

English as a new language (ENL): Used in some U.S. states to refer to programs and classes that teach students English as a new (or second or additional) language. (See *ELD* and *ESL*.)

English as a second language (ESL): Refers to programs and classes that teach students English as a second, additional, or new language. May refer to the language teaching specialists and their teaching certifications or endorsements, or may refer to the learners (i.e., ESL students). (See *ELD* and *ENL*; see also Appendix A.)

English language development (ELD): Used in some U.S. states to refer to programs and classes that teach students English as a second, additional, or new language. May refer to the language teaching specialists and their teaching certifications or endorsements. (See *ESL*.)

English language proficiency (ELP) standards: Sets of concise statements identifying the knowledge and skills that English learners are expected to know and be capable of doing in English; statement-by-statement articulations of what students are expected to learn and what schools are expected to teach. May refer to national, state, or district standards. Each U.S. state is required by the federal government to have ELP standards and related assessments. (See *ELD* and *ESL*.)

English learners (ELs)/English language learners (ELLs): Children and adults who are learning English as a second, additional, or new language, at various levels of proficiency. English learners may also be referred to as *limited English proficient* (*LEP*), *emergent bilinguals* (*EBs*), and *nonnative speakers* (*NNS*).

English-only: Used in some U.S. states, English-only refers to students whose native language is English.

English speakers of other languages (ESOL): Students whose first language is not English and who do not write, speak, or understand the language well. In some regions, this term also refers to the programs and classes for English learners.

Every Student Succeeds Act (ESSA): The federal education act passed by Congress and signed into law in December 2015, with implementation beginning in the 2017–2018 school year. ESSA holds schools accountable for the success of all their students, including English learners and other underserved populations. Each state must have standards and assessments for mathematics, reading/language arts, English language development, and science. This law replaced the No Child Left Behind Act (NCLB) of 2001.

Family engagement: A mutual partnership among families, communities, and schools built on respect and recognition on all sides of the shared responsibility that families, schools, and communities have to support student learning and success.

Feedback: A response by the teacher (or peer) to a student's output with the intent of helping the student with language learning. Common feedback types are the clarification request, repetition, recast, reformulation, explicit correction, and elicitation of self-repair/self-correction.

Formative assessment: Typically, classroom-based assessment of student performance during lessons. Takes place frequently and is ongoing throughout a lesson, involving simple but important techniques such as verbal checks for understanding, teacher-created assessments, and other nonstandardized procedures. A type of informal assessment that provides teachers with immediate information on how well a student is progressing.

Home language: The language that a learner speaks at home, usually the first language learned. Also known as *primary language*, *native language*, *first language (L1)*, and *mother tongue*.

Language form: Typically refers to aspects of the structure of a language, such as the patterns, rules, and organization of words. Comprises parts of speech, sentence formation, usage, punctuation, and so on, sometimes referred to as the *grammar* of a language.

Language function: Typically refers to the specific purpose for which language is being used—to define, compare, persuade, evaluate, and so on.

Language input: Oral or written language that is directed to the student. Differs from *language uptake*, which is the language that the student hears, perceives, and processes.

Language proficiency: A student's degree of competence in using a language for communicative and academic purposes. May be categorized as a stage of language acquisition and, in U.S. schools, is typically measured by levels.

Language transfer: A process that occurs when a student applies knowledge of one language to another, often with regard to vocabulary, sentence construction, phonology, and cognitive skills. *Positive transfer* can take place when linguistic features and learned patterns (such as cognates, letter-sound correspondences, or ways to find the main idea in a text) of a known language are similar to those in the new language and a student accurately applies them when learning the new language.

Lesson objectives (language, content, and learning strategy): Three kinds of objectives that clearly state what students will know and/or be able to do at the end of a lesson.

Limited English proficient (LEP): Describes a student who is still developing competence in using English and has limited understanding or use of written and spoken English. The federal government has used the term *LEP* in legislation, but *EL* or *ELL* is more commonly used in U.S. schools.

Long-term English learner/Long-term English language learner: A student who has been enrolled in U.S. schools for six or more years but is still designated as an English learner. Definitions and classification criteria vary by state and district, with some stipulating fewer years as an English learner or requiring that a student meet specific benchmarks of English proficiency and academic levels before redesignation as a former English learner.

Multilingualism: The use of more than one language by an individual or a community of speakers or within a geographical area. A multilingual person speaks more than one language. A multilingual community consists of a group with speakers of more than one language, but some members of the community may speak only one language.

Multi-Tiered Systems of Support (MTSS): MTSS and RtI (Response to Intervention) are often used interchangeably, but MTSS is more comprehensive, addressing student behavioral, socioemotional, and academic issues, whereas RtI focuses primarily on academic progress. See also *Response to Intervention*.

Newcomer program: Refers to specially designed academic programs for newly arrived students in U.S. schools who are at low levels of proficiency in English. Newcomers attend these programs for a limited period of time in order to develop academic English, acculturate to U.S. schools, and build content knowledge. They then typically enter an ESL/ELD or bilingual program. The programs may be located within an existing school or at a separate site. (See Appendix A.)

Next Generation Science Standards (NGSS): A set of standards for science education for students in grades K–12, adopted by nineteen states in the United States and the District of Columbia, as of 2017.

Output: Oral or written language generated by a student.

Partner languages: The home language and the target language, sometimes called the first and second languages.

Reclassification: The decision to transfer an English learner out of a language development program because the student has demonstrated that he or she has met the exit criteria. Reclassified, or former, ELs are monitored for several years after exiting the language development program.

Register: A variety of language that is associated with specific social situations. For example, academic language, legal language, baby talk.

Response to Intervention (RtI): A multi-tiered approach to the early identification and support of students with learning or behavior needs. The RtI process begins with high-quality instruction and universal screening of all children in the grade-level or content area classroom (Tier 1). Those who struggle may receive Tier 2 intervention (typically in small groups). Some may need more specialized Tier 3 intervention (usually one-on-one) to ensure successful learning.

Scaffolding: Classroom support given to assist students in learning new information and performing related tasks. Often provided by the teacher through demonstration, modeling, verbal prompts (e.g., questioning), feedback, adapted text, graphic organizers, and language frames, among other techniques. Provided to learners over a period of time but gradually modified and then removed in order to transfer more autonomy to the learner, leading to independence.

Sheltered instruction: An approach to instruction that makes academic content comprehensible for English learners while they are developing academic English proficiency. Sheltered lessons integrate language and content learning and may include culturally responsive instruction as well. Sheltered classrooms may include a mix of native English speakers and English learners or only English learners. (See Appendix A.)

Students with Interrupted Formal Education (SIFE)/Students with Limited or Interrupted Formal Education (SLIFE): Students who have significantly less education than their age-level peers. Such students may have missed years of schooling or several months over the course of several years, resulting in broad knowledge gaps that inhibit their ability to perform at grade level. Some states identify these students as being two years or more below their peers in academic performance. (Sometimes referred to as *Limited Formal Schooling* [*LFS*] students.)

Social language: A register of the English language that is also referred to as *conversational language* and is the basic language proficiency associated with fluency and vocabulary in everyday situations. Most English learners acquire social language more rapidly than academic language.

Summative assessment: A formal assessment, such as an end-of-course exam or a state standardized test. Used to measure student knowledge over an extended period of time, and may be used to measure growth in a subject area from year to year.

Target language: The language that the student is learning, which is also called *second language (L2)*, *new language*, or *foreign language*.

Translanguaging: The strategic choice to mix two or more languages to serve a specific purpose in a communicative situation or accomplish a task.

Utterance: A unit of language in spoken or written use; utterance is a broader term than *sentence* in that it includes spoken language as well as partial sentences.

Utterance frame: A partially complete spoken or written sentence that a teacher can provide to help students express ideas—for example, *I think _____ is relevant because _____; The reason I agree with _____ is that _____.* Also known as *sentence frame* or *academic language frame*.

Utterance control: The ability to produce well-formed, grammatically correct, and coherent language deliberately and purposefully when speaking or writing.

References and Further Reading

PREFACE

British Council. (2013). *The English effect: The impact of English, what it's worth to the UK, and why it matters to the world*. Manchester, England: Author.

Neeley, T. (2012, May). Global business speaks English. *Harvard Business Review*. Retrieved from https://hbr.org/2012/05/global-business-speaks -english

W3Techs. (2017). Web technology fact of the day, March 13, 2017. Retrieved June 21, 2017, from https://w3techs.com/blog/entry/fact_20170313

CHAPTER 1

Abedi, J., & Linquanti, R. (2007). *Issues and opportunities in improving the quality of large scale assessment systems for English language learners*. [Online article]. Stanford, CA: Stanford University. Retrieved from http://ell.stanford.edu/sites/default /files/pdf/academic-papers/07-Abedi%20Linquanti %20Issues%20and%20Opportunities%20FINAL.pdf

Ballantyne, K., Sanderman, A., & Levy, J. (2008). *Educating English language learners: Building teacher capacity*. Washington, DC: National Clearinghouse for English Language Acquisition. Retrieved from https://files.eric.ed.gov/fulltext /ED521360.pdf

Burr, E., Haas, E., & Ferriere, K. (2015). *Identifying and supporting English learner students with learning disabilities: Key issues in the literature and state practice* (REL 2015-086). Washington, DC: U.S. Department of Education, Institute of Education Sciences, National Center for Education Evaluation and Regional Assistance, Regional Educational Laboratory West. Retrieved from http:// ies.ed.gov/ncee/edlabs

California Department of Education (CDE). (2010). *Improving education for English learners: Research-based approaches*. Sacramento, CA: CDE Press.

Cambridge English. (2010). *Cambridge English teaching framework*. Cambridge, England: Author. Available from www.cambridgeenglish.org/teaching -framework

Canagarajah, A. S., & Wurr, A. (2011). Multilingual communication and language acquisition: New research directions. *Reading Matrix, 11*, 1–15.

Castañeda v. Pickard, 648 F. 2d 989 (5th Cir. 1981).

Cloud, N., Genesee, F., & Hamayan, E. (2009). *Literacy instruction for English language learners*. Portsmouth, NH: Heinemann.

Commission on Language Learning. (2017). *America's languages: Investing in language education for the 21st century*. Cambridge, MA: American Academy of Arts and Sciences.

Echevarría, J., Vogt, ME., & Short, D. (2017). *Making content comprehensible for English learners: The SIOP Model (5th ed.)*. Boston, MA: Pearson.

García, O., Skutnabb-Kangas, T., & Torres-Guzmán, M. (Eds.). (2006). *Imagining multilingual schools: Languages in education and glocalization*. Bristol, England: Multilingual Matters.

Horwitz, A. R., Uro, G., Price-Baugh, R., Simon, C., Uzzell, R., Lewis, S., & Casserly, M. (2009). *Succeeding with English language learners: Lessons learned from the great city schools*. Washington, DC: Council on the Great City Schools.

Keysar, B., Hayakawa, S. L., & An, S. (2011). The foreign-language effect: Thinking in a foreign tongue reduces decision biases. *Psychological Science, 23*, 661–668.

López, F., Scanlan, M., & Gundrum, B. (2013). Preparing teachers of English language learners: Empirical evidence and policy implications. *Education Policy Analysis Archives, 21*(20). Retrieved from http://epaa.asu.edu/ojs/article /view/1132

Marian, V., & Shook, A. (2013). The cognitive benefits of being bilingual. *Cerebrum*. Retrieved from http:// dana.org/Cerebrum/2012/The_Cognitive_Benefits _of_Being_Bilingual/#_ENREF_22

Murphy, D. (2014). The academic achievement of English language learners: Data for the U.S. and each of the states. *Research Brief*. Bethesda, MD: Child Trends. Retrieved from https://www .childtrends.org/wp-content/uploads/2015/07/2014 -62AcademicAchievementEnglish.pdf

National Academies of Sciences, Engineering, and Medicine. (2017). *Promoting the educational success of children and youth learning English: Promising futures*. Washington, DC: National Academies Press. Retrieved from https://doi .org/10.17226/24677

National Board for Professional Teaching Standards. (2010). *English as a new language standards (2nd ed.)*. Arlington, VA: Author.

REFERENCES FOR CHAPTER 1, *Continued*

National Center for Education Statistics [NCES]. (2017). English language learners in public schools. *The Condition of Education*. Retrieved from http://nces.ed.gov/programs/coe/indicator_cgf.asp

National Council on Teacher Quality. (2015). *2014 Teacher Prep Review: A review of the nation's teacher preparation programs*. Washington DC: Author. Retrieved from https://www.nctq.org/dmsView/Teacher_Prep_Review_2014_Report

Nieto, S., & Bode, P. (2008). *Affirming diversity: The sociopolitical context of multicultural education* (5th ed.). Boston, MA: Allyn & Bacon.

Rumberger, R. (2011). *Dropping out: Why students drop out of high school and what can be done about it*. Cambridge, MA: Harvard University Press.

Short, D., & Echevarría, J. (2016). *Developing academic language with the SIOP Model*. Boston, MA: Pearson Allyn & Bacon.

Short, D., & Fitzsimmons, S. (2007). *Double the work: Challenges and solutions to acquiring language and academic literacy for adolescent English language learners*. Report to Carnegie Corporation of New York. Washington, DC: Alliance for Excellent Education.

Smyth, T. S. (2008). Who is No Child Left Behind leaving behind? *The Clearing House: A Journal of Educational Strategies, Issues and Ideas, 81*(3), 133–137.

Sunderman, G, Kim, J., & Orfield, G. (2005). *NCLB meets school realities: Lessons from the field*. Thousand Oaks, CA: Corwin Press.

Teachers of English to Speakers of Other Languages, Inc. (TESOL). (1997). *Pre-K–12 English language standards*. Alexandria, VA: Author.

Teachers of English to Speakers of Other Languages, Inc. (TESOL). (2006). *PreK–12 English language proficiency standards: An augmentation of the World-Class Instructional Design and Assessment (WIDA) Consortium English language proficiency standards*. Alexandria, VA: Author.

TESOL International Association, Inc. (TESOL). (2013). *Implementing the Common Core State Standards for ELs: The changing role of the ESL teacher*. Alexandria, VA: Author.

TESOL International Association, Inc. (TESOL). (2018). *Standards for TESOL Pre-K–12 teacher preparation programs*. Alexandria, VA: Author.

U.S. Department of Education, Institute of Education Sciences, National Center for Education Statistics, National Assessment of Educational Progress (n.d.). *The nation's report card: 2015 mathematics and reading assessments*.

U.S. Department of Education, Office for Civil Rights, & U.S. Department of Justice, Civil Rights Division [USED & USDOJ]. (2015). *Dear colleague letter: English learner students and limited English proficient parents*. Washington, DC: Author. Retrieved from http://www2.ed.gov/about/offices/list/ocr/letters/colleague-el-201501.pdf

Valdés, G., Kibler, A., & Walqui, A. (2014). *Changes in the expertise of ESL professionals: Knowledge and action in an era of new standards*. Alexandria, VA: TESOL International Association. Retrieved from http://www.tesol.org/docs/default-source/papers-and-briefs/professional-paper-26-march-2014.pdf

Zong, J., & Batalova, J. (2015). *The limited English proficient population in the United States*. [Online journal article]. Retrieved from http://www.migrationpolicy.org/article/limited-english-proficient-population-united-states#LEP%20Children

Further Reading for Chapter 1

Bialystok, E. (2001). *Bilingualism in development: Language, literacy and cognition*. London, England: Cambridge University Press.

Castro, D. C., Ayankoya, B., & Kasprzak, C. (2011). *The new voices/Nuevas voces: Guide to cultural and linguistic diversity in early childhood*. Baltimore, MD: Brookes.

Cummins, J. (2000). *Language, power and pedagogy*. Clevedon, England: Multilingual Matters.

Gay, G. (2010). *Culturally responsive teaching: Theory, research, and practice*. New York, NY: Teachers College Press.

Nora, J., & Echevarría, J. (2017). *No more low expectations for English learners*. Portsmouth, NH: Heinemann.

Skutnabb-Kangas, T., Phillipson, R., Mohanty, A., & Panda, M. (Eds.). (2009). *Social justice through multilingual education*. Bristol, England: Multilingual Matters.

United Nations General Assembly. (1948). *Universal declaration of human rights* (217 [III] A). Paris. Retrieved from http://www.un.org/en/universal-declaration-human-rights/

CHAPTER 2

Anderson, S. R., & Lightfoot, D. W. (2002). *The language organ: Linguistics as cognitive physiology*. New York: Cambridge University Press.

Anstrom, K., DiCerbo, P., Butler, F., Katz, A., Millet, J., & Rivera, C. (2010). *A review of the literature on American English: Implications for K–12 English language learners*. Arlington, VA: George Washington University Center for Equity and Excellence in Education.

August, D., & Shanahan, T. (Eds.). (2006). *Developing literacy in second-language learners: Report of the national literacy panel on language-minority children and youth*. Mahwah, NJ: Lawrence Erlbaum.

Baker, C. (2014). *A parents' and teachers' guide to bilingualism* (4th ed.). Bristol, England: Multilingual Matters.

Baker, S., Lesaux, N., Jayanthi, M., Dimino, J., Proctor, C. P., Morris, J., Gersten, R., Haymond, K., Kieffer, M. J., Linan-Thompson, S., & Newman-Gonchar, R. (2014). *Teaching academic content and literacy to English learners in elementary and middle school* (NCEE 2014-4012). Washington, DC: National Center for Education Evaluation and Regional Assistance (NCEE), Institute of Education Sciences, U.S. Department of Education. Retrieved from http://ies.ed.gov/ncee/wwc/publications _reviews.aspx

Biemiller, A. (2010). *Words worth teaching: Closing the vocabulary gap*. Columbus, OH: SRA/McGraw-Hill.

Birdsong, D. (2016). Age of second language acquisition: Critical periods and social concerns. In E. Nicoladis & S. Montari (Eds.), *Bilingualism across the lifespan: Factors moderating language proficiency* (pp. 163–182). Berlin, Germany: De Gruyter Mouton. doi:10.1037/14939-010

Borgwaldt, S. R., & Joyce, T. (2013). Typology of writing systems. In S. R. Borgwaldt & T. Joyce (Eds.), *Typology of writing systems* (pp. 1–11). Amsterdam, Netherlands: John Benjamins.

Brown, S., & Larson-Hall, J. (2012). *Second language acquisition myths*. Ann Arbor, MI: University of Michigan Press.

Council of Europe. (2011). *Common European framework of reference for languages*. Strasbourg Cedex, France: Council of Europe. Retrieved from https://www.coe.int/en/web/common-european -framework-reference-languages/

Cloud, N., Genesee, F., & Hamayan, E. (2009). *Literacy instruction for English learners: A teacher's guide to research-based practices*. Portsmouth, NH: Heinemann.

Cummins, J. (2001). *Negotiating identities: Education for empowerment in a diverse society* (2nd ed.). Los Angeles, CA: California Association for Bilingual Education.

Custodio, B., & O'Loughlin, J. B. (2017). *Students with interrupted formal education: Bridging where they are and what they need*. Thousand Oaks, CA: Corwin.

De Angelis, G. (2007). *Third or additional language acquisition*. Clevedon, England: Multilingual Matters.

DeKeyser, R. (2010). Practice for second language learning: Don't throw out the baby with the bathwater. *International Journal of English Studies, 10*, 155–165.

DeKeyser, R. (2013). Age effects in second language learning: Stepping stones toward better understanding. *Language Learning, 63*(1), 52–67. doi:10.1111/j.1467-9922.2012.00737

DeKeyser, R. M. (Ed.). (2007). *Practice in a second language: Perspectives from applied linguistics and cognitive psychology*. New York, NY: Cambridge University Press.

Dodge, J., & Honigsfeld, A. (2014). *Core instructional routines: Go-to structures for effective literacy teaching, K–5*. Portsmouth, NH: Heinemann.

Dörnyei, Z. (2014). Motivation in second language learning. In M. Celce-Murcia, D. M. Brinton, & M. A. Snow (Eds.), *Teaching English as a second or foreign language* (4th ed., pp. 518–531). Boston, MA: National Geographic/Cengage Learning.

Dörnyei, Z., & Ushioda, E. (2011). *Teaching and researching motivation* (2nd ed.). Harlow, England: Longman.

Douglas Fir Group. (2016). A transdisciplinary framework for SLA in a multilingual world. *Modern Language Journal, 100*, S1, 19–47.

Dutro, S., & Kinsella, K. (2010). English language development: Issues and implementation at grades six through twelve. In E. Trumbull (Ed.), *Improving education for English learners: Research-based approaches* (pp. 151–207). Sacramento, CA: California Department of Education.

Echevarría, J., Vogt, ME., & Short, D. J. (2017). *Making content comprehensible for English learners: The SIOP Model* (5th ed.). Boston, MA: Pearson.

REFERENCES FOR CHAPTER 2, *Continued*

Ellis, R. (2017). Oral corrective feedback in L2 classrooms. In H. Nassaji & E. Kartchava (Eds.), *Corrective feedback in second language teaching and learning: Research, theory, applications, implications*. New York, NY: Routledge.

Ellis, R., & Shintani, N. (2014). *Exploring language pedagogy through second language acquisition research*. New York, NY: Routledge.

Every Student Succeeds Act of 2015, Pub. L. No. 114-95 § 114 Stat. 1177 (2015–2016).

Fairbairn, S., & Jones-Vo, S. (2010). *Differentiating instruction and assessment for English language learners: A guide for K–12 teachers*. Philadelphia, PA: Caslon.

Fang, Z., & Schleppegrell, M. J. (2008). *Reading in secondary content areas: A language-based pedagogy*. Ann Arbor, MI: University of Michigan Press.

Gardner, R. C. (1985). *Social psychology and second language learning: The role of attitudes and motivation*. London, England: Edward Arnold.

García, O., Ibarra Johnson, S., & Seltzer, K. (2017). *The translanguaging classroom: Leveraging student bilingualism for learning*. Philadelphia, PA: Caslon.

Gibbons, P. (2009). *English learners, academic literacy, and thinking*. Portsmouth, NH: Heinemann.

Gibbons, P. (2015). *Scaffolding language, scaffolding learning: Teaching English learners in the mainstream classroom* (2nd ed.). Portsmouth, NH: Heinemann.

Gottlieb, M., Katz, A., Ernst-Slavit, G. (2009). *Paper to practice: Implementing TESOL's pre-K–12 English language proficiency standards*. Alexandria, VA: TESOL International Association.

Grabe, W. (2009). *Reading in a second language: Moving from theory to practice*. New York, NY: Cambridge University Press.

Greenberg Motamedi, J. (2015). *Time to reclassification: How long does it take English learner students in Washington Road Map Districts to develop English proficiency?* (REL 2015-092). Washington, DC: U.S. Department of Education, Institute of Education Sciences, National Center for Education Evaluation and Regional Assistance, Regional Educational Laboratory Northwest. Retrieved from http://ies.ed.gov/ncee/edlabs

Hadaway, N. L., & Young, T. A. (2010). *Matching books and readers: Helping English learners in grades K–6*. New York, NY: Guilford.

Helman, L. (Ed.). (2016). *Literacy development with English learners: Research-based instruction in grades K–6*. New York, NY: Guilford.

Herrera, S. G., Perez, D. R., & Escamilla, K. (2014). *Teaching reading to English language learners: Differentiated literacies* (2nd ed.). Boston, MA: Allyn & Bacon.

Hoover, J. J., Baca, L. M., & Klinger, J. K. (Eds.) (2016). *Why do English learners struggle with reading? Distinguishing language acquisition from learning disabilities* (2nd ed.). Thousand Oaks, CA: Corwin.

Jeon, E-Y., & Day, R. R. (2016). The effectiveness of ER on reading proficiency: A meta-analysis. *Reading in a Foreign Language, 28*(2), 246–265.

Johnson, K. (1995). *Understanding communication in second language classrooms*. Cambridge, England: Cambridge University Press.

Klinger, J. K., Almanza de Schonewise, E., de Onís, C., Méndez Barletta, L. (2016). Misconceptions about the second language acquisition process. In J. J. Hoover, L. M. Baca, & J. K. Klinger (Eds.), *Why do English learners struggle with reading? Distinguishing language acquisition from learning disabilities* (pp. 57–81). Thousand Oaks, CA: Corwin.

Kohnert, K. (2013). *Language disorders in bilingual children and adults* (2nd ed.). San Diego, CA: Plural Publishing.

Krashen, S. (1985). *The input hypothesis: Issues and implications*. New York, NY: Longman.

Krekeler, C. (2006). Language for special academic purposes (LSAP) testing: The effect of background knowledge revisited. *Language Testing, 23*(1), 99–130. doi:10.1191/0265532206lt323oa

Lesaux, N., Koda, K., Siegel, L., & Shanahan, T. (2006). Development of literacy. In D. August & T. Shanahan (Eds.), *Developing literacy in second-language learners: Report of the national literacy panel on language-minority children and youth* (pp. 75–122). Mahwah, NJ: Lawrence Erlbaum.

Lightbown, P., & Spada, N. (2014). *How languages are learned* (4th ed.). New York, NY: Oxford University Press.

Lin, Z. (2002). Discovering EFL readers' perception of prior knowledge and its roles in reading comprehension. *Journal of Research in Reading, 25*(2), 172–190.

Lynch, E. W. (2011). Developing cross-cultural competence. In E. W. Lynch & M. J. Hanson (Eds.), *Developing cross-cultural competence: A guide for working with children and their families* (4th ed., pp. 41–78). Baltimore, MD: Brookes Publishing.

Lyster, R., & Saito, K. (2010). Oral feedback in classroom SLA. *Studies in Second Language Acquisition, 32*, 265–302. doi:10.1017/S0272263109990520

Mackey, A., Abbuhl, R., & Gass, S. M. (2012). Interactionist approach. In S. Gass & A. Mackey (Eds.), *The Routledge handbook of second language acquisition* (pp. 7–23). New York, NY: Routledge.

Muir, C., & Dörnyei, Z. (2013). Directed motivational currents: Using vision to create effective motivational pathways. *Studies in Second Language Learning and Teaching, 3*(3), 357–375.

Muñoz, C. (2011). Input and long-term effects of starting age in foreign language learning. *International Review of Applied Linguistics in Language Teaching, 49*(2), 113–133.

Murray, G., Gao, X., & Lamb, T. (Eds.). (2011). *Identity, motivation and autonomy in language learning.* Bristol, England: Multilingual Matters.

Nagy, W. E., & Scott, J. A. (2000). Vocabulary processes. In M. Kamil, P. Mosenthal, P. D. Pearson, & R. Barr (Eds.), *Handbook of reading research* (vol. 3, pp. 269–284). Mahwah, NJ: Lawrence Erlbaum.

Nakanishi, T. (2015). A meta-analysis of extensive reading research. *TESOL Quarterly, 49*(1), 6–37. doi:10.1002/tesq.157

Nassaji, H., & Kartchava, E. (Eds.). (2017). *Corrective feedback in second language teaching and learning: Research, theory, applications, implications.* New York, NY: Routledge.

Nation, I. S. P. (2008). *Teaching vocabulary: Strategies and techniques.* Boston, MA: Heinle/Cengage Learning.

Nation, I. S. P., & Webb, S. (2011). *Researching and analyzing vocabulary.* Boston, MA: Heinle.

National Academies of Sciences, Engineering, and Medicine (NASEM). (2017). *Promoting the educational success of children and youth learning English: Promising futures.* Washington, DC: National Academies Press. Retrieved from https://doi.org/10.17226/24677

Norton, B. (2013). *Identity and language learning.* Bristol, England: Multilingual Matters.

Nutta, J. W., Strebel, C., Mokhtari, K., Mihai, F. M., & Crevecoeur-Bryant, E. (2014). *Educating English learners: What every classroom teacher needs to know.* Cambridge, MA: Harvard Education Press.

Ó Laoire, M., & Singleton, D. (2009). The role of prior knowledge in L3 learning and use: Further evidence of psychotypological dimensions. In L. Aronin & B. Hufeisen (Eds.), *The exploration of multilingualism: Development of research on L3, multilingualism and multiple language acquisition* (pp. 79–102). Amsterdam, Netherlands: John Benjamins.

Pavlenko, A., & Norton, B. (2007). Imagined communities, identity, and English language teaching. In J. Cummins & C. Davidson (Eds.), *International handbook of English language teaching* (pp. 669–680). New York, NY: Springer.

Rex, L. A., & Green, J. L. (2008). Classroom discourse and interaction: Reading across the traditions. In B. Spolsky & F. M. Hult (Eds.), *The handbook of educational linguistics* (pp. 571–584). Malden, MA: Blackwell.

Rutgers, D., & Evans, M. (2015). Bilingual education and L3 learning: Metalinguistic advantage or not? *International Journal of Bilingual Education & Bilingualism.* Retrieved from http://dx.doi.org/10.1080/13670050.2015.1103698

Sanderson, G. (2004). Existentialism, globalisation and the cultural other. *International Education Journal, 4*(4), 1–20.

Sato, M., & Ballinger, S. (2016). Understanding peer interaction: Research synthesis and directions. In M. Sato & S. Ballinger (Eds.), *Peer interaction and second language learning: Pedagogical potential and research agenda* (pp. 1–30). Amsterdam, Netherlands: John Benjamins. doi:10.1075/lllt.45.01int

Saunders, W. M., & O'Brien, G. (2006). Oral language. In F. Genesee, K. Lindholm-Leary, W. M. Saunders, & D. Christian (Eds.), *Educating English language learners* (pp. 14–63). New York: Cambridge University Press.

Schmitt, N., Jiang, X., & Grabe, W. (2011). The percentage of words known in a text and reading comprehension. *Modern Language Journal, 95*, 26–43.

Short, D., & Echevarría, J. (2016). *Developing academic language with the SIOP Model.* Boston, MA: Pearson Allyn & Bacon.

REFERENCES FOR CHAPTER 2, *Continued*

Swain, M., & Suzuki, W. (2008). Interaction, output, and communicative language learning. In B. Spolsky & F. M. Hult (Eds.), *The handbook of educational linguistics* (pp. 557–570). Malden, MA: Blackwell.

Teachers of English to Speakers of Other Languages, Inc. (TESOL). (2006). *PreK–12 English language proficiency standards: An augmentation of the World-Class Instructional Design and Assessment (WIDA) Consortium English language proficiency standards*. Alexandria, VA: Author.

Turkan, S., Bicknell, J., & Croft, A. (2012). *Effective practices for developing the literacy skills of English language learners in the English language arts classroom*. [Research Report ETS RR-12-03]. Princeton, NJ: ETS. Retrieved from http://files.eric.ed.gov/fulltext/EJ1109828.pdf

Valdés, G., Kibler, A., & Walqui, A. (2014). *Changes in the expertise of ESL professionals: Knowledge and action in an era of new standards*. Alexandria, VA: TESOL International Association. Retrieved from http://www.tesol.org/docs/default-source/papers-and-briefs/professional-paper-26-march-2014.pdf

Van Patten, B., & Williams, J. (2014). *Theories in second language acquisition* (2nd ed.). New York, NY: Routledge.

Vardell, S. M., Hadaway, N. L., & Young, T. A. (2006). Matching books and readers: Selecting literature for English learners. *The Reading Teacher, 59*(8), 734–741.

Weingarten, R. (2013). Comparative graphematics. In S. R. Borgwaldt & T. Joyce (Eds.), *Typology of writing systems* (pp. 13–39). Amsterdam, Netherlands: John Benjamins.

WIDA. (2012). *2012 amplification for the English language development standards, Kindergarten–grade 12*. Madison, WI: Author.

Williams, M., Mercer, S., & Ryan, S. (2015). *Exploring psychology in language learning and teaching*. New York, NY: Oxford University Press.

Zwiers, J. (2014). *Building academic language: Grades 5–12* (2nd ed.). San Francisco, CA: Jossey-Bass.

CHAPTER 3

Andrade, M. S., & Evans, N. W. (2013). *Principles and practices for response in second language writing*. New York, NY: Routledge.

August, D., & Hakuta, K. (Eds.). (2002). *Educating language minority children*. Washington, DC: National Academy Press.

Chamot, A. U. (2009). *The CALLA handbook: Implementing the cognitive academic language learning approach* (2nd ed.). Boston, MA: Pearson.

Cohen, A. D., & Macaro, E. (Eds.). (2008). *Language learner strategies: 30 years of research and practice*. Oxford, England: Oxford University Press.

Dewey, J. (1933). *How we think: A restatement of the relation of reflective thinking to the educative process*. Boston, MA: D. C. Heath.

Dove, M. G., & Honigsfeld, A. (2017). *Co-teaching for English learners*. Thousand Oaks, CA: Corwin.

Dweck, C. S. (2006). *Mindset: The new psychology of success*. New York, NY: Random House.

Echevarría, J., Vogt, ME., & Short, D. (2017). *Making content comprehensible for English learners: The SIOP Model* (5th ed.). Boston, MA: Pearson.

Gibbons, P. (2014). *Scaffolding language scaffolding learning: Teaching English language learners in the mainstream classroom* (2nd ed.). Portsmouth, NH: Heinemann.

Gay, G. (2010). *Culturally responsive teaching: Theory, research, and practice* (2nd ed.). New York, NY: Teachers College Press.

Harklau, L. (1994). ESL versus mainstream classes: Contrasting L2 learning environments. *TESOL Quarterly, 28*: 241–272.

Harklau, L. (2000). From the "good kids" to the "worst": Representations of English language learners across educational settings. *TESOL Quarterly, 34*: 35–67.

Herrell, A., & Jordan, M. (2008). *Fifty strategies for teaching English language learners* (3rd ed.). Upper Saddle River, NJ: Pearson/Merrill Prentice Hall.

Larrivee, B. (2000). Transforming teaching practice: Becoming the critical reflective teacher. *Reflective Practice, 1*(3), 293–307.

Lave, J., & Wenger, E. (1991). *Situated learning: Legitimate peripheral participation*. Cambridge, England: Cambridge University Press.

Levine, L. N., Lukens, L., & Smallwood, B. A. (2013). *The GO TO Strategies: Scaffolding options for teachers of English language learners. K–12*. Retrieved from http://www.cal.org/what-we-do/projects/project-excell/the-go-to-strategies

Levine, L. N., & McCloskey, M. (2013). *Teaching English language and content in mainstream classes: One class, many paths* (2nd ed.). Boston, MA: Pearson.

Lyster, R., & Saito, K. (2010). Interactional feedback as instructional input. *Language, Interaction, and Acquisition, 1*(2), 276–297.

Mayer, R. E. (1992). Cognition and instruction: Their historic meeting within educational psychology. *Journal of Educational Psychology, 84*, 405–412.

Michaels, S., O'Connor, M. C., Williams Hall, M., & Resnick, L. B. (2013). *Accountable talk sourcebook: For classroom conversation that works.* Retrieved from http://ifl.pitt.edu/index.php /educator_resources/accountable_talk

Nieto, S., & Bode, P. (2011). *Affirming diversity: The sociopolitical context of multicultural education* (6th ed.). Boston, MA: Pearson.

Rivera, C. (2006). *Using test accommodations to level the playing field for ELLs.* Presentation at the LEP Partnership Meeting, Washington, DC, August 28–29, 2006.

Saunders, W., & Goldenberg, C. (1999). The effects of instructional conversations and literature logs on limited and fluent English proficient students' story comprehension and thematic understanding. *Elementary School Journal, 99*, 277–301.

Schon, D. A. (1990). *The reflective turn: Case studies in and on educational practice.* New York, NY: Teachers College Press, Columbia University.

Short, D., & Echevarría, J. (2016). *Developing academic language with the SIOP Model.* Boston, MA: Pearson Allyn & Bacon.

Staehr Fenner, D. (2016). *The preparation of the ESL educator in the era of college- and career-readiness standards, A summary of the TESOL International Association convening February 2016.* Alexandria, VA: TESOL International Association.

Swain, M., & Lapkin, S. (1995). Problems in output and the cognitive processes they generate: A step towards second language learning. *Applied Linguist, 16(3):* 371–391.

Teachers of English to Speakers of Other Languages, Inc. (TESOL). (2006). *PreK–12 English Language Proficiency Standards: An augmentation of the World-Class Instructional Design and Assessment (WIDA) Consortium English language proficiency standards.* Alexandria, VA: Author.

TESOL International Association, Inc. (TESOL). *Standards for TESOL Pre-K–12 teacher preparation programs.* Alexandria, VA: Author.

Tomlinson, C. A. (2014). *The differentiated classroom: Responding to the needs of all learners* (2nd ed.). Alexandria, VA: Association for Supervision and Curriculum Development.

Valdés, G., Kibler, A., & Walqui, A. (2014). *Changes in the expertise of ESL professionals: Knowledge and action in an era of new standards.* Alexandria, VA: TESOL International Association. Retrieved from http://www.tesol.org/docs/default-source /papers-and-briefs/professional-paper-26-march -2014.pdf

Vogt, ME., & Echevarría, J. (2008). *99 ideas and activities for teaching English learners with the SIOP Model.* Boston, MA: Pearson Allyn & Bacon.

Wood, D., Bruner, J., & Ross, G. (1976). The role of tutoring in problem solving. *Journal of Child Psychology and Psychiatry,* 17: 89–100.

Zimmerman, B. J., & Schunk, D. H. (2012). An essential dimension of self-regulated learning. In D. H. Schunk & B. J. Zimmerman (Eds.), *Motivation and self-regulated learning: Theory, research, and applications* (pp. 1–30). New York, NY: Routledge.

Further Reading for Chapter 3

Reading about the Common Core State Standards (CCSS):

De Oliveira, L. C., Klassen, M., & Maune, M. (Eds.). (2015). *The Common Core State Standards in Language Arts, grades 6–12.* Alexandria, VA: TESOL International Association.

Spycher, P. (Ed.). (2014). *The Common Core State Standards in English Language Arts for English language learners, grades K–5.* Alexandria, VA: TESOL International Association.

In addition, the TESOL International series on CCSS and English learners includes the following:

The Common Core State Standards in Mathematics, grades K–8

The Common Core State Standards in Mathematics, high school

The Common Core State Standards for Literacy in History/Social Studies, Science, and Technical Subjects for English language learners, grades 6–12

Other suggested reading:

Gottlieb, M., & Ernst-Slavit, G. (2014). *Academic language in diverse classrooms: Definitions and contexts.* Thousand Oaks, CA: Corwin.

A companion six-book series includes the following titles:

Academic language in diverse classrooms: English language arts, grades K–2

REFERENCES FOR CHAPTER 3, *Continued*

> *Academic language in diverse classrooms: Mathematics, grades K–2*

> *Academic language in diverse classrooms: English language arts, grades 3–5*

> *Academic language in diverse classrooms: Mathematics, grades 3–5*

> *Academic language in diverse classrooms: English language arts, grades 6–8*

> *Academic language in diverse classrooms: Mathematics, grades 6–8*

Honigsfeld, A., & Dove, M. G. (2010). *Collaboration and co-teaching strategies for English learners*. (2010). Thousand Oaks, CA: Corwin.

Saunders, W., & Goldenberg, C. (2010). Research to guide English language development instruction. In California Department of Education (Ed.), *Improving education for English learners: Research-based approaches* (pp. 21–81). Sacramento, CA: CDE Press

Takanishi, R., & Le Menestrel, S. (Eds.). (2017). *Promoting the educational success of children and youth learning English: Promising futures*. Washington, DC: National Academies Press.

Tools and resources for providing ELs with a language assistance program. https://www2.ed.gov/about/offices/list/oela/english-learner-toolkit/index.html

CHAPTER 4

Baker, S., Lesaux, N., Jayanthi, M., Dimino, J., Proctor, C.P., Morris, J., Gersten, R., Haymond, K., Kieffer, M. J., Linan-Thompson, S., & Newman-Gonchar, R. (2014). *Teaching academic content and literacy to English learners in elementary and middle school* (NCEE 2014-4012). Washington, DC: National Center for Education Evaluation and Regional Assistance (NCEE), Institute of Education Sciences, U.S. Department of Education. Retrieved from http://ies.ed.gov/ncee/wwc/publications_reviews.aspx

Commission on Language Learning. (2017). *America's languages: Investing in language education for the 21st century*. Cambridge, MA: American Academy of Arts and Sciences.

Cloud, N., Genesee, F., & Hamayan, E. (2009). *Literacy instruction for English language learners: A teacher's guide to research-based practices*. Portsmouth, NH: Heinemann.

Custodio, B., & O'Loughlin, J. (2017). *Students with interrupted formal education: Bridging where they are and what they need*. Thousand Oaks, CA: Corwin.

Echevarría, J., Vogt, ME., & Short, D. (2017). *Making content comprehensible for English learners: The SIOP Model (5th ed.)*. Boston, MA: Pearson.

Every Student Succeeds Act of 2015, Pub. L. No. 114-95 § 114 Stat. 1177 (2015–2016).

Genesee, F. (n.d.). *The home language: An English language learner's most valuable resource*. [Online article]. Retrieved from http://www.colorincolorado.org/article/home-language-english-language-learners-most-valuable-resource

Honigsfeld, A., & Dove, M. G. (2010). *Collaboration and co-teaching: Strategies for English learners*. Thousand Oaks, CA: Corwin.

Horwitz, A. R., Uro, G., Price-Baugh, R., Simon, C., Uzzell, R., Lewis, S., & Casserly, M. (2009). *Succeeding with English language learners: Lessons learned from the great city schools*. Washington, DC: Council on the Great City Schools.

McGraner, K., & Saenz, L. (2009). *Preparing teachers of English language learners*. Washington DC: National Comprehensive Center for Teacher Quality.

National Board for Professional Teaching Standards. (2016). *English as a new language*. Retrieved from http://boardcertifiedteachers.org/sites/default/files/ECYA-ENL.pdf

National Center for Education Statistics. (2017, March). *English language learners in public schools*. Retrieved from https://nces.ed.gov/programs/coe/indicator_cgf.asp

National Education Association. (n.d.). NCLB stories: Florida. Retrieved from http://www.nea.org/home/nclbvoices_Florida.html

National Education Association. (2015). *All in! How educators can advocate for English language learners*. Washington, DC: Author. Retrieved from https://www.nea.org/assets/docs/ADV104_DODSON_All_In_How_Educators_Can_Advocate_for_ELLs.pdf

National Governors Association Center for Best Practices & Council of State School Officers (2010). *Common core state standards for English language arts & literacy in history/social studies, science, and technical subjects*. Washington, DC: Author. Retrieved from http://www.corestandards.org

No Child Left Behind Act of 2001. Pub. L. No. 107-110 § 115, Stat. 1425 (2002).

Nutta, J. W., Mokhtari, K., and Strebel, C. (2012). *Preparing every teacher to reach English learners: A guide for teacher educators*. Cambridge, MA: Harvard Education Press.

Short, D., & Echevarría, J. (2016). *Developing academic language with the SIOP Model*. Boston, MA: Pearson Allyn & Bacon.

Soto, I. (2012). *ELL shadowing as a catalyst for change*. Thousand Oaks, CA: Corwin.

Staehr Fenner, D. (2013). *TESOL Report: The changing role of the ESL teacher*. Retrieved from http://www.colorincolorado.org/blog/tesol-report-changing-role-esl-teacher

Staehr Fenner, D. (2014). *Advocating for English learners: A guide for educators*. Thousand Oaks, CA: Corwin.

TESOL International Association, Inc. (TESOL). (2018). *Standards for TESOL Pre-K–12 teacher preparation programs*. Alexandria, VA: Author.

Thomas, W. P., & Collier, V. P. (2003). The multiple benefits of dual language, *Educational Leadership, 61*(2), pp. 61–64. Retrieved from http://www.ascd.org/ASCD/pdf/journals/ed_lead/el200310_thomas.pdf

U.S. Department of Education, Office for Civil Rights & U.S. Department of Justice, Civil Rights Division [USED & USDOJ]. (2014). *Information on the rights of all children to enroll in school: Questions and answers for states, school districts and parents*. Washington, DC: Author. Retrieved from http://images.politico.com/global/2014/05/08/plyler_qa_-_05-05-14.html

U.S. Department of Education, Office for Civil Rights & U.S. Department of Justice, Civil Rights Division [USED & USDOJ]. (2015). *Dear colleague letter: English learner students and limited English proficient parents*. Washington, DC: Author. Retrieved from http://www2.ed.gov/about/offices/list/ocr/letters/colleague-el-201501.pdf

Zwiers, J. (2008). *Building academic language: Essential practices for content classrooms*. San Francisco, CA: John Wiley & Sons.

Further Reading for Chapter 4

National Education Association. (2015). *All in! How educators can advocate for English language learners*. Washington, DC: Author.

CHAPTER 5

Burr, E., Haas, E., & Ferriere, K. (2015). *Identifying and supporting English learner students with learning disabilities: Key issues in the literature and state practice* (REL 2015–086). Washington, DC: U.S. Department of Education, Institute of Education Sciences, National Center for Education Evaluation and Regional Assistance, Regional Educational Laboratory West. Retrieved from: http://ies.ed.gov/ncee/edlabs

Echevarría, J., Vogt, ME., & Short, D. (2017). *Making content comprehensible for English learners: The SIOP Model (5th ed.)*. Boston, MA: Pearson.

Educational Testing Service. (2009). *Guidelines for the assessment of English language learners*. Princeton, NJ: Author.

Every Student Succeeds Act of 2015, Pub. L. No. 114-95 § 114 Stat. 1177 (2015–2016).

Genesee, F., & Lindholm-Leary, K. (2012). The education of English language learners. In K. R. Harris, S. Graham, T. Urdan, C. B. McCormick, G. M. Sinatra, & J. Sweller (Eds.), *APA educational psychology handbook* (pp. 499–526). Washington, DC: APA Books.

Gonzalez, N., Moll, L., & Amanti, C. (Eds.). (2005). *Funds of knowledge: Theorizing practices in households, communities, and classrooms*. New York, NY: Routledge.

Honigsfeld, A., & Dove, M. G. (2010). *Collaboration and co-teaching: Strategies for English learners*. Thousand Oaks, CA: Corwin. (See "Administrators' Role" sections in Chapters 2–8.)

Lave, J., & Wenger, E. (1991). *Situated learning: Legitimate peripheral participation*. Cambridge, England: University of Cambridge Press.

Louie, B.Y., & Knuth, R. (2016). Home visit tips for ELLs. *Principal, 95*(4), 44. Retrieved from https://www.naesp.org/sites/default/files/LouieKnuth_MA16.pdf

Movit, M., Petrykowska, I., & Woodruff, D. (2010). Using school leadership teams to meet the needs of English language learners. *Information Brief*. Washington, DC: National Center on Response to Intervention. Retrieved from http://ea.niusileadscape.org/docs/FINAL_PRODUCTS/LearningCarousel/Using_School_Leadership_Teams.pdf

Seddon, J. (2015). School counselor support for the academic, career, personal, and social needs of ELL students. *Culminating projects in community psychology, counseling and family therapy, paper 8*. St. Cloud, MN: St. Cloud State University.

REFERENCES FOR CHAPTER 5, *Continued*

Short, D., Vogt, ME., & Echevarría, J. (2017). *The SIOP Model for administrators* (2nd ed.). New York, NY: Pearson.

Stepanek, J., & Raphael, J. (2010). Creating schools that support success for English language learners. *Lessons learned, 1*(2), 1–4. Portland, OR: Education Northwest. Retrieved from http://files.eric.ed.gov/fulltext/ED519412.pdf

Theoharis, G., & O'Toole, J. (2011). Leading inclusive ELL: Social justice leadership for English language learners. *Educational Administration Quarterly 47*(4), 646–688.

U.S. Department of Education, Office for Civil Rights & U.S. Department of Justice, Civil Rights Division [USED & USDOJ]. (2015). *Dear colleague letter: English learner students and limited English proficient parents*. Washington, DC: Author. Retrieved from http://www2.ed.gov/about/offices/list/ocr/letters/colleague-el-201501.pdf

Young, J. W. (2008). Ensuring valid content tests for English language learners. *ETS R&D Connections* (No. 8). Princeton, NJ: Educational Testing Service.

Further Reading for Chapter 5

Soltero, S. W. (2011). *Schoolwide approaches to educating ELLs: Creating linguistically and culturally responsive K–12 schools*. Portsmouth, NH: Heinemann.

Soto, I. (2012). *ELL shadowing as a catalyst for change*. Thousand Oaks, CA: Corwin.

Zacarian, D. (2011). *Transforming schools for English learners: A comprehensive framework for school leaders*. Thousand Oaks, CA: Corwin.